Let's Eat
Mediterranean
Tonight

CW01091240

Let's Eat

Mediterranean
Tonight

Jean Conil

foulsham
LONDON • NEW YORK • TORONTO • SYDNEY

foulsham

The Publishing House, Bennetts Close
Cippenham, Berkshire, SL1 5AP

ISBN 0-572-01884-3

Copyright © 1995 W. Foulsham & Co. Ltd.

Typeset in Great Britain by Typesetting Solutions, Slough, Berks.
Printed in Great Britain by Cox & Wyman Ltd., Reading, Berks.

Contents

Introduction

Olive oil is indispensible to the cuisine of Greece, southern France, Italy, Spain, Portugal and the islands of the Mediterranean. And it is a major contributing factor in the healthy diet of the peoples of this region.

Variations of the same recipe can be found in many of these countries, each having received a different influence — Greek cookery has been influenced by Turkish cuisine, and spices and a taste for vegetarian dishes have come through the Mediterranean ports from Africa and the East.

Hot countries are perfect for open-air barbecues, and grilled fish, poultry and meat are favourites in many Mediterranean countries. Eaten with a variety of sauces and salads, they are ideal for a simple family celebration or a relaxing meal with friends.

The flavours of herbs, garlic, onions and oriental spices can often be detected — no one could accuse food from this region of being bland. Wine is another major ingredient and is a particular favourite of the French, Italians and Spanish.

Vegetables and fruit are grown in abundance, and though the quality of meat cannot be said to be as good as that in the cooler northern countries, where grazing is better, a range of high-quality delicatessen goods is produced in all the countries whose shores bound the Mediterranean; and the region has well earned its reputation for succulent hams and spicy salamis.

Italy, of course, heads the field with its pasta and Spain with its olive oil and tapas. The French are famed for their hors d'oeuvres and the Greeks for their Mezzes. In Mediterranean cookery you will find the undeniable flavour of the region in all of the dishes — sometimes garlic, onions and tomatoes, always olive oil and, occasionally the subtle flavour of saffron or cumin will surprise the taste buds.

Enjoy trying the recipes and sampling the end result, but if you want a quick and easy introduction to the region, then all you need are a fig, an olive, a piece of crusty bread and a good cheese, all washed down with a robust young wine.

Chapter

1

Basic Cold Sauces

Basic Cold Sauces

All these sauces can be used for salads, cold or hot fish, egg, pasta, soups or poultry dishes as indicated under the recipes. Garlic should always be chopped and liquidised to a paste.

Original mayonnaise, made by blending together egg yolk and oil, is probably as old as the olive tree, for it seems that all the meridional countries where olive oil is produced include this sauce with all its variations. Today mayonnaise can be made with any kind of oil other than olive oil, but with meridional dishes only olive oil should be used.

Spanish Mayonnaise
Mayonnaise Espagnole

Ingredients
2 egg yolks
Salt and white pepper
25 ml/½ tsp sweet ready-made yellow mustard
300 ml/½ pt/1¼ cups slightly tepid olive oil
15 ml/1 tbsp sherry vinegar
Juice of ½ lemon

Method

1. Place the egg yolks, seasoning and mustard in a clean mixing bowl. Start whisking gently then pour the oil in a small thread until the mixture begins to thicken. Continue to whisk the sauce until all the oil is used.

2. Heat 15 ml/1 tbsp of sherry vinegar and stir it in to make the sauce smoother and white. Add the lemon juice.

Serves 4

Preparation time: 4 mins

Green Sauce
(Salsa Verde)

Ingredients
2 green tomatoes, seeded
6 mint leaves, finely chopped
6 watercress leaves
6 spinach leaves
2 slices green chilli (chili)
15 ml/1 tbsp parsley leaves
300 ml/½ pt/1¼ cups mayonnaise
Salt and pepper

Method
1. Liquidise the green seeded tomatoes, mint, cress, spinach, chilli and parsley leaves to a purée with 250 ml/8 fl oz/1 cup of the mayonnaise.

2. Blend the remaining mayonnaise into the green sauce.

3. Check and adjust the seasoning.

Serves 4

Preparation time: 4 mins

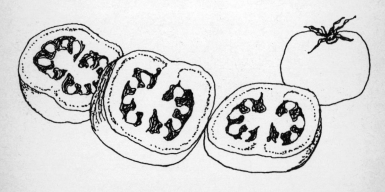

Garlic Mayonnaise
(Aioli)

This a real garlic mayonnaise but it can also be made with
soaked bread, garlic and oil only. (See Panada à l'Ail.)

Ingredients
4 garlic cloves, chopped
250 ml/8 fl oz/1 cup mayonnaise

Method
1. Blend the chopped garlic with half the mayonnaise and
liquidise it to a fine purée. Pass this through a sieve (strainer)
and blend in the remaining mayonnaise.

Serves 4

Preparation time: 4 mins

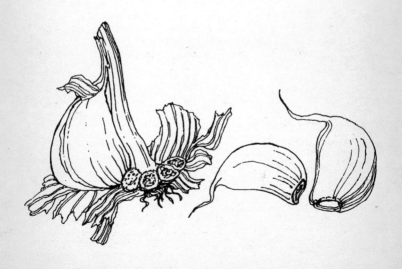

'Mayonnaise' with Breadcrumbs (Panada à l'Ail)

Ingredients
100 g/4 oz/2 cups white breadcrumbs
30 ml/2 tbsp hot water
4 garlic cloves, finely chopped
150 ml/5 fl oz/⅔ cup olive oil
Juice of ½ lemon
Salt and pepper

Method
1. Soak the bread in the boiling water for a few minutes.

2. Press the excess moisture out.

3. In a mortar, pound the garlic to a paste, add the bread and mix well.

4. Gradually whisk in the oil to obtain a smooth emulsion. (This can be done with an electric blender.) Add the lemon juice.

5. Check and adjust the seasoning.

<u>Serves 4</u>

Preparation time: 10 mins

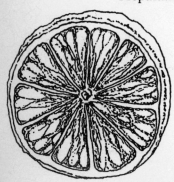

Basil Sauce
(Pistou Sauce)

Ingredients
30 ml/2 tbsp basil leaves
50 g/2 oz/½ cup pine nuts
3 garlic cloves
Salt
50 g/2 oz/½ cup grated Parmesan cheese
50 g/2 oz/½ cup grated Gruyère cheese
150 ml/5 fl oz/⅔ cup olve oil

Method

1. In a mortar, pound or mash the basil leaves, pine nuts and garlic with a pinch of salt.

2. Add the two grated cheeses and pound until you have a paste.

3. Gradually stir in the oil to obtain a smooth mixture. (This can also be made in a blender.)

Serves 4

Preparation time: 18 mins

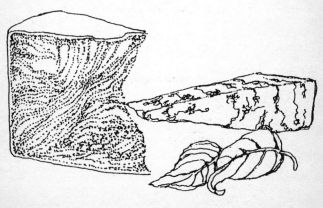

Almond Mayonnaise (Sauce Amandine)

Ingredients

75 g/3 oz/¾ cup blanched whole almonds
30 ml/2 tbsp boiling water
150 ml/5 fl oz/⅔ cup mayonnaise
50 g/2 oz/¼ cup fromage frais
15-30 ml/1-2 tbsp hot water
Salt and pepper

Method

1. Liquidise the almonds and water to a paste.

2. Blend this paste with the mayonnaise and fromage frais.

3. Adjust the texture with a little hot water.
Season to taste.

Serves 4

Preparation time: 5 mins

Vinaigrette Provençale

Ingredients
15 ml/1 tbsp wine vinegar
30 ml/2 tbsp basil leaves
1 small sprig of parsley
2 garlic cloves
1 shallot
2.5 ml/½ tsp Dijon mustard
Juice and grated rind of 1 lemon
Salt and black pepper
45 ml/3 tbsp olive oil

Method
1. Liquidise all the ingredients except the oil.

2. Stir the oil into the made sauce.

Serves 4

Preparation time: 5 mins

Sweet and Sour Sauce
(Agrodolce Sauce)

Ingredients
75 ml/5 tbsp sweet white wine
15 ml/1 tbsp wine vinegar
15 ml/1 tbsp sugar
15 ml/1 tbsp honey
Juice of 1 lemon
75 ml/5 tbsp tomato juice
Salt and pepper
For the garnish:
50 g/2 oz/⅓ cup sultanas (golden raisins)
30 ml/2 tbsp parsley
1 small pickled gherkin, chopped

Method
1. Blend all the ingredients in a bowl and leave for 1 hour before use.

2. Sprinkle over the garnish.

Serves 4

Preparation time: 5 mins

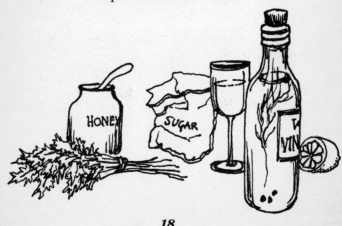

Fresh Tomato Sauce
(Coulis de Tomates)

Ingredients
60 ml/4 tbsp oil
60 ml/4 tbsp chopped onion
2 garlic cloves, chopped
30 ml/2 tbsp plain (all-purpose) flour
4 large tomatoes, skinned, seeded and chopped
Salt, pepper and 5 ml/1 tsp sugar

Method

1. In a pan, stir-fry the onion in the oil for 2 minutes without browning.

2. Add the garlic and cook for 30 seconds.

3. Blend in the flour to absorb surplus oil.

4. Add the chopped tomatoes.

5. Cook for 4 minutes. Season to taste then pass through a sieve (strainer).

Serves 4

Preparation time: 8 mins

Basque Sauce
(Sauce Basquaise)

Ingredients
30 ml/2 tbsp oil
1 red (bell) pepper, seeded and cut in strips
4 button mushrooms, sliced
150 ml/5 fl oz/⅔ cup white wine
120 ml/4 fl oz/½ cup water
1 stock cube, chicken, fish or beef depending
on the requirement
300 ml/½ pt/1¼ cups Fresh Tomato Sauce (see page 19)
15 ml/1 tbsp fresh or 7.5 ml/½ tbsp dried tarragon

Method
1. Heat the oil in a pan and stir-fry the red pepper strips for 5 minutes.

2. Add the mushrooms and cook for 1 minute.

3. Add the wine, water and stock cube and boil for 10 minutes.

4. Blend in the Fresh Tomato sauce.

5. Add the tarragon.

Basquaise can be used for fish, veal or poultry. Instead of a stock cube, you can use 5 ml/1 tsp of yeast extract or Marmite.

Serves 4

Preparation time: 8 mins

Mediterranean White Sauce
Sauce Blanc

Ingredients
25 g/1 oz/2 tbsp vegetable margarine
25 g/1 oz/¼ cup plain (all-purpose) flour
600 ml/1 pt/2½ cups milk or almond milk
1 garlic clove, chopped
Salt and white pepper

Method
1. Heat the margarine in a saucepan, add the flour and cook for 1 minute until the mixture looks like wet sand.

2. Gradually add the cold milk, stirring with a spoon or spatula to avoid lumps.

3. Bring to the boil and simmer with the garlic for 5 minutes.

4. Season to taste. Then pass the sauce through a sieve (strainer). Use the sauce for chicken, veal, fish, vegetables and pasta. It can be enriched with 75 ml/5 tbsp of cream and 1 egg yolk or the grated rind of 1 lemon when used with chicken.

Serves 8

Preparation time: 8 mins

Quick Variations on White Sauces

Herb Sauce
To 600 ml/1 pt/2½ cups white sauce, add 30 ml/2 tbsp fresh chopped herbs (parsley, basil, chervil, cress, chives).

Cheese Sauces
Blue Cheese Sauce: Add 50g/2 oz/½ cup grated Roquefort or any blue cheese to 600 ml/1 pt/2½ cups white sauce together with 30 ml/2 tbsp cream.

Savoy Cheese Sauce: Add 50 g/2 oz/½ cup grated yellow cheese to 600 ml/1 pt/2½ cups white sauce.

Mornay Sauce: Add 50 g/2 oz/½ cup grated Gruyère cheese, plus
1 egg yolk and 50 ml/3½ tbsp/¼ cup single (light) cream to 600 ml/1 pt/
2½ cups white sauce.

Mushroom Sauce
Add 50g/2 oz/½ cup sliced white mushrooms boiled 2 minutes in 75 ml/5 tbsp/⅓ cup of dry white wine to 600 ml/1 pt/2½ cups white sauce. Wild mushrooms may be used for a stronger flavour.

The flavour can be changed by using fish liquor, chicken stock, veal stock or stock cubes in the ratio of 1 part stock to 4 parts white sauce.

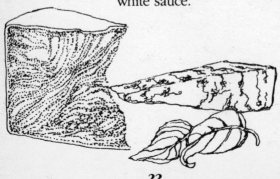

Chapter

2

Salads and Starters

Salads and Starters

There is a magical attraction in the multicoloured salads and other foods that the Italians call 'Antipasti', the Greek and Turks 'Mezze', the French 'Hors d'Oeuvre' and the Spanish 'Tapas'.

The food of the countries bordering the northern and eastern shores of the Mediterranean is essentially that of the peasant; it is good home cooking or *la cucina casalinga*. I could sum it up in three Italian words: bordetto, polenta and pasta. The soups are a kaleidoscope of vegetables, legumes and pasta. A complete meal where very little fish or meat is included except to add a little flavour; whereas the antipasti could contain any of the semi-tropical produce of that entire Mediterranean region, even oriental spices and exotic vegetables brought over by sailors travelling from the east and north Africa.

The Romans invented foie gras by overfeeding their geese on fresh figs. Pigs fed on chestnuts provide us with a vast range of delicatessen products: you cannot have hors d'oeuvres variés without a salami or saucisson as we call it in France. And when you start to think of sausages you enter a realm of limitless complexities — every village seems to have its own kind of 'charcuterie'. The smoked salamis studded with pistachio, black and green pepper-corns, a slice of Mortadella with black olives and pickled onions make a hearty hors d'oeuvre. You can get varieties with garlic and orange peel, as the Abruzzi sausages; liver sausages flavoured with honey or hot pimentos, and the Zampone looking like a pig's foot.

In all the seaside resorts you will find the best quality smoked ham, often served with melon or fresh figs. Jambon de Bayonne or Parma ham are served in every café, and not just the upmarket restaurants.

The tingling challenges of antipasti are so inviting that it is easy to be tempted into opening a tin of baby artichoke hearts or artichoke bottoms, ready to be eaten with salad dressing.

And look at the range of canned fish, the varieties of Spanish olives, and the enormous range of salamis of all sizes and tastes which in no time at all can help you to prepare a Mediterranean platter *al fresco* with no cooking at all.

And finally we have the fragrant and herby green salads, and the vegetables and mushrooms which, after being blanched for a few seconds, can be marinated in sweet and sour sauces. A selection of any of these foods will transport you to those European countries bordering the Mediterranean.

Anchovy and Olive Spread (Tapenade)

Ingredients
50 g/2 oz canned anchovies in oil
1 garlic clove, chopped
15 ml/1 tbsp pickled capers
6 black olives, stoned
50 g/2 oz/½ cup goat's cheese
15 ml/1 tbsp vinegar
1 small onion, chopped
4 slices rustic bread

Method
1. Pound all the ingredients except the bread to a paste, including the oil in the can.

2. Toast the bread on both sides. Spread the paste on each slice and serve as an appetiser.

Serves 4

Preparation time: 5 mins

Red Mullet Salad with Capers and Fennel (Salad Antiboise)

Ingredients
450 g/1 lb fresh red mullet, filleted and cut in four pieces
30 ml/2 tbsp olive oil
225 g/8 oz new potatoes, boiled and sliced
120 ml/4 fl oz/½ cup Vinaigrette Provençale
(see page 17)
Curly leaved lettuce
30 ml/2 tbsp pickled capers
1 fennel bulb, thinly sliced
Salt and black pepper

Method
1. Brush oil over fish fillets and grill for 5 minutes.

2. Toss the potatoes in Provençal dressing.

3. Arrange the salad leaves on four plates and place the fish on top.

4. Sprinkle the capers over the fish and cover with thin slices of fennel. Arrange the potatoes around.

5. Sprinkle with salt and black pepper.

Serves 4

Preparation time: 10 mins
Cooking time: 8 mins

Salad Niçoise

Ingredients
8 lettuce leaves
225 g/8 oz canned tuna fish
225 g/8 oz cooked green beans (haricots verts)
2 tomatoes, sliced
8 black olives, stoned (pitted)
1 red (bell) pepper, seeded and cut into thin strips
4 canned anchovy fillets
4 hard-boiled (hard-cooked) eggs
120 ml/4 fl oz/½ cup Vinaigrette Provençal (see page 17)

Method
1. Arrange the lettuce leaves on the plates. Put the tuna in the centre with the green beans on top. Arrange the tomatoes, olives and pepper strips around the tuna.

2. Cut the anchovies into thin strips and the eggs into slices.

3. Arrange the eggs as a border with anchovy strips across them.

4. Drizzle on some salad dressing just before the salad is to be served.

All the ingredients should be arranged attractively and not mixed up in one bowl as in the old style.

Serves 4

Preparation time: 8 mins

Spanish Salad
Salade Espagnole

This fish salad is popular all over the Mediterranean. Smoked fish is particularly favoured in hot countries for its salt content and its keeping quality. Any smoked fish can be used: cod, haddock, halibut, tuna or mackerel.

Ingredients
225 g/8 oz smoked cod
225 g/8 oz boiled new potatoes
125 ml/4 fl oz/½ cup Garlic Mayonnaise (see page 13)
Grated rind and juice of 1 lemon
Green lettuce leaves
1 green (bell) pepper, seeded and cut into rings
1 red onion, cut into thin rings

Method
1. Poach the smoked cod in water for 8 minutes. Cool and flake the fish.

2. Cut the potatoes into cubes and mix with the mayonnaise and lemon rind.

3. Arrange the lettuce leaves around the edge of four plates and the potato mixture in the centre. Top up with fish and the rings of pepper and onions in alternate rows.

4. Squeeze a little lemon juice over the fish.

Serves 4

Preparation time: 8 mins
Cooking time: 5 mins

Mediterranean Rice Salad
(Salade de Riz Méditerranée)

Ingredients
150 g/5 oz/scant ⅔ cup long-grain rice
4 strands saffron
30 ml/2 tbsp hot water
120 ml/4 fl oz/½ cup Garlic Mayonnaise (see page 13)
1 red (bell) pepper, seeded and diced
8 olives, stoned (pitted)
150 g/5 oz/1¼ cups cooked, peeled prawns (shrimp)
Radicchio leaves

Method

1. Boil the rice for 18 minutes. Drain and rinse under the tap until cold. Drain again and pat dry in a cloth.

2. Infuse the saffron in the hot water, strain and add the liquid to the mayonnaise.

3. Blend the garlic mayonnaise with the rice, pepper and olives.

4. Arrange the radicchio leaves on four plates. Place rice mixture on top and decorate with prawns. Do not mix the prawns with the rice for better presentation.

Serves 4

Preparation time: 5 mins
Cooking time: 18 mins

Vegetable Salad Provençale
(Insalata di Legumi)

Ingredients
30 ml/2 tbsp olive oil
1 carrot, cut in strips 3 mm/⅛ in thick
1 turnip, cut into strips 3 mm/⅛ in thick
3 (bell) peppers, 1 green, 1 red, 1 yellow, cut into thick strips
1 onion, cut into strips
15 ml/1 tbsp honey
Salt and pepper
120 ml/4 fl oz/½ cup Vinaigrette Provençale
(see page 17)

Method

1. Heat the oil in a shallow pan and stir-fry the vegetables for 2 minutes.

2. Add the honey and seasoning. Cool.

3. When cold, toss in Provençale dressing.

Serves 4

Preparation time: 4 mins
Cooking time: 5 mins

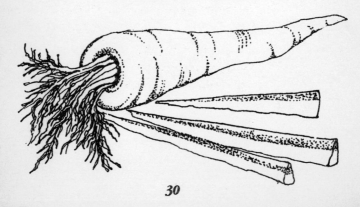

Noodle Salad
(Insalata di Taglioni)

Ingredients
225 g/8 oz thin noodles (taglioni)
30 ml/2 tbsp olive oil
1 red onion, cut into strips
Salt and black pepper
15 ml/1 tbsp honey
Juice and grated rind of 1 lemon
Fresh field mushrooms, sliced
1 pickled gherkin, cut into small strips
30 ml/2 tbsp pine nuts or pistachio nuts, skinned

Method
1. Boil the noodles for 8 minutes. Drain.

2. In a large frying pan (skillet), heat the oil and stir-fry the onion
for 1 minute.

3. Add the noodles and toss for a few minutes.

4. Season with salt, pepper, honey, lemon juice and rind.

5. Add the mushrooms and cook for 1 minute.

6. Stir in the gherkin and nuts. Serve.

Serves 4

Preparation time: 5 mins
Cooking time: 8 mins

Leek Salad
(Salade de Poireaux)

Ingredients
**16 small leeks, trimmed, washed and tied
in 4 bundles with string
Salt
300 ml/½ pt/1¼ cups Sweet and Sour Sauce (see page 18)
50 g/2 oz/½ cup flaked almonds, toasted**

Method
1. Boil the leeks in salted water for 8 minutes. Drain and press moisture out gently.

2. Trim off the green part, leaving the leeks whole.

3. Marinate the cooked leeks in sweet and sour sauce for 2 hours.

4. Serve on plates with some of the sauce, allowing 4 per portion.

5. Sprinkle flaked almonds over the top.

Serves 4

Preparation time: 5 mins
Cooking time: 8 mins

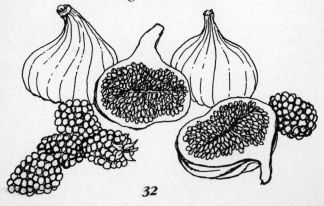

Cucumber Salad with Yoghurt and Mint (Tzatziki)

Ingredients
1 cucumber, peeled, split and seeded
Salt
120 ml/4 fl oz/½ cup Greek yoghurt
15 ml/1 tbsp honey or sugar
Lettuce leaves
8 mint leaves, chopped

Method
1. Slice the cucumber slantwise. Sprinkle over a little salt and leave for 10 minutes. Rinse off and drain.

2. Combine the yoghurt, honey or sugar and cucumber.

3. Arrange the lettuce leaves on four plates and spoon the cucumber on top. Sprinkle with chopped mint.

Serves 4

Preparation time: 15 mins

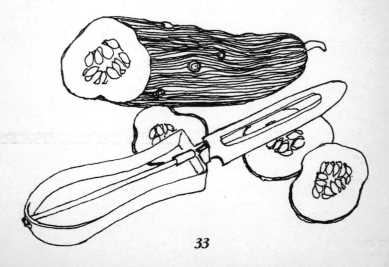

New Potato Salad in Lemon Sauce (Patates di Lemoni)

Ingredients
450 g/1 lb new potatoes, boiled and sliced
120 ml/4 fl oz/½ cup Vinaigrette Provençale dressing
(see page 17) using lemon juice instead of vinegar
Juice and grated rind of 1 lemon
Lettuce leaves
2 hard-boiled (hard-cooked) eggs, chopped
8 large olives, stoned (pitted) and chopped
4 small slices red water melon

Method
1. Place the cooked potatoes in a bowl. Mix the dressing with the lemon juice and rind and stir into the potatoes.

2. Arrange the mixture on the lettuce leaves on four plates and sprinkle chopped eggs and olives on top.

3. Decorate with thin slices of red melon pulp and the black seeds, which are edible and rich in protein.

Serves 4

Preparation time: 5 mins
Cooking time: 20 mins

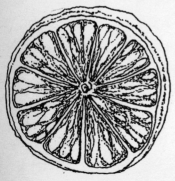

Tomato Salad with Smoked Tuna Fish (Salade de Tomates Riviera)

Ingredients
**4 large tomatoes, 100 g/4 oz each
1 large red onion, cut into thin rings
4 slices of smoked tuna fish, cut into small strips
75 ml/5 tbsp Vinaigrette Provençale (see page 17)
1 garlic clove, chopped
30 ml/2 tbsp chopped parsley**

Method
1. Cut the tomatoes in slices laterally and arrange on four large plates.

2. Top with onion rings and place strips of smoked tuna fish around the edge.

3. Drizzle with Provençale dressing and sprinkle chopped garlic and parsley on top.

Serves 4

Preparation time: 5 mins

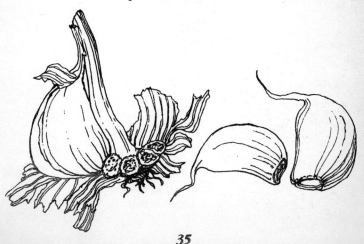

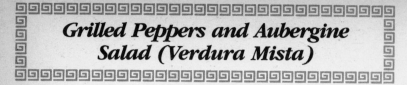

Grilled Peppers and Aubergine Salad (Verdura Mista)

Ingredients
12 (bell) peppers (allow 1 red, 1 green and 1 yellow pepper per person)
Oil for brushing
2 aubergines (eggplants)
Salt
45 ml/3 tbsp seasoned flour
125 ml/4 fl oz/½ cup Vinaigrette Provençale (see page 17)
30 ml/2 tbsp sesame seeds
2 bunches of watercress

Method
1. Cut the peppers in half and remove the membranes and seeds.

2. Brush with oil and grill for 2 minutes on the outer side. Remove skins when they blister.

3. Cut the aubergines into thin slices lengthwise. Sprinkle with salt, leave for 5 minutes then rinse. Drain well. Rub in seasoned flour, brush with oil and grill (broil) for 2 minutes on one side only.

4. Cut the peppers into strips. Mix in a bowl and toss in the dressing. Season to taste.

5. Place two slices of grilled aubergine on each plate. Sprinkle sesame seeds over and surround the mixture with peppers, watercress or other green leaves.

Serves 4

Preparation time: 5 mins
Cooking time: 6 mins

Grilled Sardines
(Sardines Grillées Tunisienne)

Sardines are exceedingly rich in calcium as the bones are edible. You do not have to gut fresh sardines and it is better to leave the scales on too. Just wash them in salted icy water.

Ingredients
20 fresh sardines
45 ml/3 tbsp seasoned flour plus 5 ml/1 tsp salt
and 1.5 ml/¼ tsp black pepper
45 ml/3 tbsp olive oil
75 ml/5 tbsp Vinaigrette Provençale (see page 17)

Method
1. Wash and dry the sardines. Cover them in seasoned flour then dip in olive oil.

2. Grill (broil) for 2 minutes on each side. Allow five sardines per portion. Serve a sauceboat of Vinaigrette Provençale separately.

Serves 4

Preparation time: 4 mins
Cooking time: 4 mins

Stuffed Vine Leaves
(Dolmades à la Grecque)

Ingredients
16 young vine leaves with stems removed
For the stuffing:
150 g/5 oz/scant ⅔ cup cream cheese
25 g/1 oz/½ cup white breadcrumbs
50 g/2 oz/⅓ cup sultanas (golden raisins)
1 egg, beaten
Salt and pepper
Juice and grated rind of 1 lemon
25 g/1 oz/½ cup white breadcrumbs
For the coating:
60 ml/4 tbsp seasoned flour
1 egg, beaten
45 ml/3 tbsp water
100 g/4 oz/2 cups brown breadcrumbs
50 g/2 oz/½ cup flaked almonds
Oil for shallow frying

Method
1. Boil the vine leaves for 3 minutes, rinse and cool on ice cubes. Pat dry.

2. In a bowl, combine the cream cheese, breadcrumbs, sultanas, and egg, seasoning, lemon juice and grated rind. Divide the mixture into 16 balls.

3. Wrap each ball in a vine leaf. Roll in seasoned flour then in beaten egg mixed with the water and finally in brown breadcrumbs mixed with nibbed almonds.

4. Heat the oil in a pan and deep-fry the balls, a few at a time, for 1 minute or until golden brown. Serve with tomato salad.

Serves 4

Preparation time: 5 mins
Cooking time: 5 mins

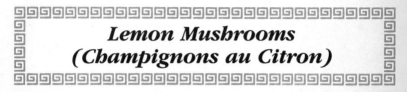

Lemon Mushrooms
(Champignons au Citron)

Ingredients
**300 ml/½ pt/1¼ cups Sweet and Sour Sauce
(see page 18)
450 g/1 lb button mushrooms
1 fennel bulb, sliced
1 lemon sliced**

Method
1. Bring the sweet and sour sauce to the boil and cook the mushrooms and fennel for 3 minutes.

2. Cool all the ingredients and chill with slices of lemon on top.

3. Serve as an hors d'oeuvre with green salad.

Serves 4

Preparation time: 5 mins
Cooking time 4 mins

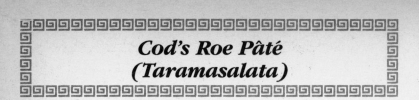

Cod's Roe Pâté (Taramasalata)

Ingredients
150 g/5 oz/¾ cup smoked cod's roe
1 small shallot, finely chopped
1 garlic clove, finely chopped
150 ml/5 fl oz/⅔ cup olive oil
Juice and finely grated rind of 1 lemon
Salt and white pepper
¼ tsp paprika

Method
1. Remove the skin around the cod's roe. Scrape the roe well.

2. Place the roe in a bowl with the finely chopped shallot and garlic.

3. Gradually whisk in the oil until the mixture is creamy and thick, as for mayonnaise. Add the lemon juice and grated rind.

4. For a smoother paste, pass the mixture through a blender or a sieve (strainer).

5. Season to taste and add paprika for colour.

Serves 4

Preparation time: 5 mins

Broad Beans with Mozzarella
(Fava a Sorpresa)

Ingredients
225 g/8 oz/2 cups shelled broad (lima) beans
1 garlic clove, chopped
120 ml/4 fl oz/½ cup single (light) cream
Salt, pepper, grated nutmeg
225 g/8 oz Mozzarella cheese, cut in 4 slices

Method
1. Boil the broad beans for 8 minutes in salted water. Drain and rinse in cold water. Remove the rough skin to expose the very green nut-like bean.

2. Add the garlic to the cream and bring to the boil.

3. Season and reheat the beans in this sauce for 3 minutes.

4. Place the whole mixture into four individual ramekin dishes. Put a slice of Mozzarella on top and grill (broil) until the cheese has melted.

You could also place a poached egg on top for a more substantial starter.

Serves 4

Preparation time: 6 mins
Cooking time: 8 mins

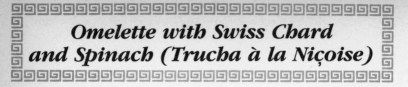

Omelette with Swiss Chard and Spinach (Trucha à la Niçoise)

This omelette is cooked flat, without folding it in half. The ingredients will serve four. Either cook four individual omelettes or two large ones and cut each in half.

Ingredients
225 g/8 oz Swiss chard leaves
225 g/8 oz leaf spinach
90 ml/6 tbsp olive oil
8 eggs
50 g/2 oz/½ cup grated Gruyère cheese
1 garlic clove, chopped
45 ml/3 tbsp chopped parsley
60 ml/4 tbsp chopped (snipped) chives
Salt and pepper

Method
1. Trim the chard and spinach leaves. Cut off the stems. Wash three times. Drain well. Heat 30 ml/2 tbsp of the oil in a large pan and cook the leaves for 4 minutes. Stir from time to time but keep the saucepan covered with a lid. When cooked, drain well and press the moisture out of the leaves by squeezing in a cloth. Chop the leaves coarsely.

2. Beat 4 eggs in a bowl. Add half the cheese, the chopped garlic, parsley and chives. Season to taste. Blend half of the cooked leaves into this egg mixture.

3. Heat 30 ml/2 tbsp of remaining oil in an 18 cm/7 in omelette pan. When smoking hot, pour the mixture in. Let it cook for 1 minute then scramble it a little and let it cook for a further 1 minute. Turn the omelette, either by tossing it or by placing a plate on top, turning the omelette on to it, then slipping the uncooked side onto the pan, with a little more oil.

Cook for 1 more minute like a thick pancake. Repeat the operation for the second omelette.

Serves 4

Preparation time: 5 mins
Cooking time: 3-4 mins

Feta Cheese Salad
(Feta Salata)

Ingredients
225 g/8 oz Feta cheese, cut into 2 cm/¾ in cubes
For the sauce:
4 tomatoes, skinned, seeded and coarsely chopped
12 stuffed olives
1 garlic clove
Salt and pepper
120 ml/4 fl oz/½ cup olive oil
Juice and finely grated rind of 1 lemon
For the garnish:
Mixture of chicory (endive), coriander (cilantro)
and red and green curly salad leaves

Method
1. Place all the sauce ingredients in a bowl. Marinate the feta cubes in this sauce and chill for 24 hours.

2. Serve in individual bowls with salad leaves in separate containers.

Serves 4

Preparation time: 5 mins

Scrambled Eggs with Aubergine (Oeufs à l'Arlesienne)

Ingredients
1 aubergine (eggplant), peeled and diced
60 ml/4 tbsp olive oil
1 shallot, chopped
2 garlic cloves, chopped
15 ml/1 tbsp sesame seeds
1 tomato, skinned, seeded and chopped
2 eggs, beaten
Salt, pepper and a good pinch of chilli (chili) pepper
50 g/2 oz/½ cup grated Gruyère cheese

Method
1. Sprinkle salt over the aubergine and leave for 30 minutes. Rinse off and pat dry.

2. Heat the oil and stir-fry the aubergine for 4 minutes in a wok or frying pan (skillet).

3. Add the shallot, garlic, sesame seeds and tomato. Cook for a further 2 minutes.

4. Stir the eggs into this mixture for 1 minute until scrambled.

5. Season to taste and coarsely mash the mixture.

6. Put into individual ramekin dishes (custard cups), sprinkle with grated Gruyère and brown under the grill (broiler).

7. Serve with granary bread.

Serves 4

Preparation time: 5 mins
Cooking time: 5 mins

Chapter

3

Soups

Soups

Southern soups have one thing in common: they all contain cereal in the form of pasta, rice or bread. The words minestrone and minestra come from the Latin word ministrare, which once signified that pasta was used in the soup. So soup does not replace the dry pasta course; it *is* the pasta course.

A good example of the importance of minestrone can be found in Genoa, which claims to have invented that mighty soup. Peasants all over the world are accustomed to keeping a pot simmering on the stove, into which is put whatever farm produce comes to hand. The Genoese minestrone contains cabbage, courgettes (zucchini), fava beans, red beans, string beans, tomato, aubergines (eggplants), celery, onion, garlic, olive oil, herbs and any kind of pasta you fancy — especially tagliatelle, ditalini, vermicelli, penne and rigatoni. But the average minestrone should have fresh vegetables, some dried legumes, aromatic vegetables such as celery, fennel, onion, garlic, pasta of your choice, or rice and even a little bacon. The best known type is the Milanese minestrone. The selection that follows is an example of the most popular soups in the whole of the Mediterranean countries.

Spicy Sausage and Green Cabbage Soup (Caldo Verde)

Ingredients
60 ml/4 tbsp olive oil
1 onion, chopped or sliced
450 g/1 lb potatoes, peeled, washed and thinly sliced
½ green cabbage, cored and leaves shredded,
washed and drained
Salt and pepper
1 litre/1¾ pts/4¼ cups water
1 chorizo spiced sausage or garlic sausage, sliced

Method
1. Heat the oil in a saucepan and stir-fry the onion, without colouring, for 2 minutes.

2. Add the sliced potatoes and cabbage. Season to taste and stir in the water. Boil for 15-20 minutes.

3. Serve with slices of cooked spiced or garlic sausage, or poached egg.

Serves 6

Preparation time: 5 mins
Cooking time: 20 mins

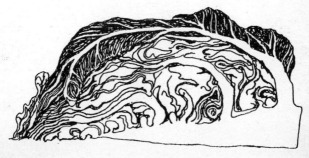

Green Lentil Soup
(Sopa de Lentejas)

Ingredients
225 g/8 oz green lentils
60 ml/4 tbsp olive oil
1 onion, chopped
1 carrot, chopped
2 rashers (slices) of rindless bacon, chopped
1 green (bell) pepper, seeded and chopped
½ green chilli (chili), seeded and chopped
2 beef or vegetable stock cubes
1.5 litres/2½ pts/6 cups water
3 garlic cloves, chopped
4 large tomatoes, skinned, seeded and chopped
Salt and pepper

Method
1. Soak the green lentils for 1 hour.

2. Heat the oil in a large saucepan and stir-fry the onion, carrot, bacon, pepper and chilli for 4 minutes.

3. Crumble the stock cubes into the water and add to the saucepan with the lentils, garlic and tomatoes.
Boil for 20-25 minutes.

4. Pass the soup through a sieve (strainer) or liquidise to a thin purée. Check the seasoning. Serve with crusty granary bread.

Serves 6

Preparation time: 5 mins
Cooking time: 30 mins

Sicilian Asparagus Soup
(Minestra Siciliana)

Ingredients
225 g/8 oz green asparagus
1.5 litres/2½ pts/6 cups water
75 g/3 oz/⅓ cup long-grain rice
45 ml/3 tbsp olive oil
4 rindless bacon rashers (slices), diced
3 shallots, chopped
45 ml/3 tbsp chopped parsley
50 g/2 oz/½ cup grated Gruyère or Parmesan cheese
Salt and pepper

Method

1. Scrape the asparagus lightly. Tie up in a bunch and boil in the water for 8 minutes. Strain and save the water.

2. Boil the rice in the asparagus water for 20 minutes.

3. Heat the oil in a pan and stir-fry the bacon and shallots for 2 minutes.

4. Cut the cooked asparagus into 4 cm/1½ in pieces.

5. Complete the soup by mixing the rice and liquid into the fried bacon, asparagus, chopped parsley and grated cheese. Season to taste.

Serves 6

Preparation time: 5 mins
Cooking time: 12 mins

Vegetable and Bacon Soup
(Minestrone con il Lardo)

Ingredients
1 onion, chopped
¼ green cabbage, shredded, washed and drained
1 celery stick (rib), sliced
1 potato, peeled, cut into chips and sliced across
1 carrot, peeled and cut into 2.5 cm/1 in pieces
75 g/3 oz/¾ cup fresh or frozen small peas
75 g/3 oz/¾ cup French beans, topped and tailed
and cut into small pieces
2 tomatoes, skinned, seeded and chopped
1.5 litres/2½ pts/6 cups water
60 ml/4 tbsp olive oil
6 rindless bacon rashers (slices), cut in small cubes
50 g/2 oz/60 ml/4 tbsp thin spaghetti or vermicelli
2 chicken stock cubes
Salt and pepper
6 sprigs basil, chopped
30 ml/2 tbsp chopped parsley or chervil
1 garlic clove, finely chopped
50 g/2 oz/½ cup grated Parmesan cheese

Method
1. Clean, wash and cut all the vegetables to the same size.

2. Heat the oil in a large saucepan and fry (sauté) the bacon
and onion for 2 minutes, then add other vegetables.

3. Keep on stirring for 4 minutes to develop the flavour,
then add the water.

4. Bring to the boil and cook for 15 minutes.

5. Add the pasta, stock cubes and seasoning. Simmer for
another 10 minutes.

6. Sprinkle with chopped herbs and garlic at the last moment (1 minute before the end of cooking time).

7. Adjust seasoning. Serve the grated cheese separately.

Serves 6-10

Preparation time: 10 mins
Cooking time: 35 mins

Chilled Tomato and Cucumber Soup (Panzarella)

Ingredients
4 large tomatoes, skinned, seeded and chopped
1 cucumber, peeled, seeded and chopped
6 basil leaves, chopped
6 shallots or spring onions (scallions), chopped
60 ml/4 tbsp olive oil
4 slices of granary bread, cut into cubes
30 ml/2 tbsp wine vinegar
15 ml/1 tbsp sugar
Salt and pepper
1 litre/1¾ pts/4¼ cups water

Method
1. In a large earthernware bowl marinate all ingredients overnight in a refrigerator.

2. Pass through a moulinette or liquidise to a thin purée.

3. Check seasoning and serve chilled. The thickness can be adjusted by using less water.

Serves 4

Preparation time: 5 mins

Bean Soup
(Zuppa di Faghioli)

The easiest method to prepare a bean soup in 5 minutes is to liquidise a tin of baked beans in tomato sauce and thin it down with a cup of milk. Cooking beans takes a long time. The haricot beans must be soaked overnight and they will take 2 hours to cook gently in water, but a little less time if boiled in distilled water.
The simplified method makes use of haricot beans canned in plain brine.

Ingredients
60 ml/4 tbsp oil
3 rindless bacon rashers (slices), chopped
1 onion, chopped
2 garlic cloves, chopped
225 g/8 oz/1⅓ cups haricot beans, cooked
1 potato, peeled and diced
30 ml/2 tbsp tomato purée (paste)
1.5 litres/2½ pts/6 cups water
Salt and pepper
1 glass port wine
For the garnish:
100 g/4 oz/1 cup French beans, topped and tailed, cut into small pieces and boiled separately for 8 minutes

Method
1. Heat the oil in a large saucepan. Stir-fry the bacon until crisp.

2. Add the onion, garlic and cooked haricot beans.

3. Stir for 3 minutes then add potato, tomato purée and water.

4. Bring to the boil and simmer for 25 minutes.

5. Pass through a sieve (strainer) or liquidise it.

6. Reheat the soup, season to taste. Add the port wine and boiled French beans as garnish.

Serves 6

Preparation time: 5 mins
Cooking time: 25 mins

Almond and Garlic Soup (Sopa de Ajo)

Ingredients
100 g/4 oz/1 cup almonds, skinned
½ green chilli (chili)
6 garlic cloves, chopped
45 ml/3 tbsp olive oil
100 g/4 oz/2 cups white breadcrumbs
1 litre/1¾ pts/4¼ cups boiling water
Salt and pepper

Method
1. In a mortar, pound the almonds, chilli and garlic to a paste, adding the oil a little at a time.

2. Blend the breadcrumbs into the mixture.

3. Gradually stir in the boiling water and season to taste.

4. Reboil and simmer gently for 4 minutes.

The mixture can also be liquidised, reboiled and strained.

Serves 4

Preparation time: 5 mins
Cooking time: 10 mins

Vegetable Soup with Fish and Basil Dumplings (Soupe au Pistou)

Ingredients
60 ml/4 tbsp olive oil
1 leek, trimmed, washed and thinly sliced
1 carrot, peeled and sliced
1 potato, peeled, cut in chips and sliced across
1 litre/1¾ pts/4¼ cups water
15 ml/1 tbsp tomato purée (paste)
3 strands saffron

For the dumplings:
225 g/8 oz fish fillets (cod, haddock, hake), skinned
6 basil leaves, chopped
15 ml/1 tbsp chopped parsley
1 garlic clove, chopped
1 egg, beaten
75 g/3 oz/1½ cups breadcrumbs
Salt and pepper
75 g/3 oz/¾ cup grated cheese (any kind)

Method
1. Stir-fry the vegetables in half the oil for 4 minutes until lightly coloured. Add the water, tomato purée and saffron. Bring to the boil and simmer for 15 minutes.

2. Wash and dry the fish. Chop it finely and blend it in a bowl with the basil, parsley, garlic, beaten egg and breadcrumbs to obtain a paste. Season to taste.

3. Divide the mixture into four dumplings. Heat the remaining oil in a frying pan (skillet) and fry (sauté) the dumplings on both sides for 2 minutes. This will harden them.

4. To serve, place each dumpling in an individual earthernware soup bowl. Fill up with soup. Sprinkle over grated cheese and bake in a hot oven for 12 minutes at 200°C/400°F/gas mark 6.

Serves 4

Preparation time: 5 mins
Cooking time: 15 minutes

Chicken Soup with Lemon
(Soupe de Volaille au Citron)

Ingredients
2 chicken breasts with skin left on
60 ml/4 tbsp olive oil
1 onion, chopped
30 ml/2 tbsp plain (all-purpose) flour
1 litre/1¾ pts/4¼ cups water
15 ml/1 tbsp chopped lemon grass
Thinly grated rind of 1 lemon
Salt and pepper
2 egg yolks
15 ml/1 tbsp cornflour (cornstarch)
45 ml/3 tbsp water
45 ml/3 tbsp lemon juice
15 ml/1 tbsp sugar or honey

Method
1. Cut the chicken meat into small cubes.

2. Heat the oil in a saucepan and stir-fry the chicken and onion for 4 minutes on a low heat.

3. Sprinkle the flour into the saucepan to absorb surplus oil and fill with water. Add the lemon grass and grated lemon rind. Bring to the boil and simmer for 20 minutes. Season to taste.

4. Mix the egg yolks, cornflour and the water in a large bowl. Gradually add 250 ml/8 fl oz/1 cup of the soup liquid and pour this egg mixture onto the chicken soup. Bring it to the boil and simmer for 4 minutes while stirring.

5. Check the seasoning. Add the lemon juice and finally the sugar or honey.

Serves 4

Preparation time: 5 mins
Cooking time: 25 mins

Chilled Melon Soup (Sopa Melone)

Ingredients
1 ripe cantaloupe melon with orangey pulp
Juice of 2 oranges
Juice of 1 lemon
300 ml/½ pt/1¼ cups medium sherry
100 g/4 oz ice cubes
50 g/2 oz/¼ cup sugar
5 ml/1 tsp ground ginger
8 mint leaves

Method
1. Cut the melon in half. Remove the seeds and rind. Cut one half into cubes and reserve the other.

2. Blend the orange and lemon juice in a bowl with the sherry and half of the melon pulp. Add the ice cubes and liquidise the mixture. Add the sugar and ginger.

3. Serve in glasses with a garnish of melon cubes and fresh mint leaves.

Serves 4

Preparation time: 5 mins

Maltese Pumpkin Soup
(Soppa Tal-Qara-Ahmar)

Ingredients
45 ml/3 tbsp olive oil
1 large red onion, chopped
450 g/1 lb pumpkin, peeled, seeded and cut
into small cubes
1 litre/1¾ pts/4¼ cups water
30 ml/2 tbsp tomato purée (paste)
Salt and pepper
1.5 ml/¼ tsp cinnamon
75 g/3 oz/½ cup semolina (cream of wheat)
45 ml/3 tbsp olive oil
75 g/3 oz/¾ cup grated cheese
(any kind of hard cheese can be used)

Method
1. Heat the oil in a large saucepan and stir-fry the onion
for 2 minutes.

2. Add the pumpkin and simmer for 2 minutes, then add the
water and tomato purée. Boil for 20 minutes until tender.

3. Sieve (strain) the soup into another pan and season to taste.

4. Mix the semolina, oil and grated cheese in a cup. Add this
mixture to the hot soup, whisking to avoid lumps. Cook for
5 more minutes, then check seasoning and add cinnamon if liked.

The soup can be enriched with milk or cream.

Serves 4

Preparation time: 5 mins
Cooking time: 30 mins

Chapter

4

Pasta

Pasta

Southern European meals are made up of many pasta dishes, either in soup forms or in sauces. Made with eggs or without, pasta is often enriched with cheese and is a valuable source of protein. In fact, a plain egg noodle is richer in protein than bread, rice or maize.

Pasta comes in a variety of shapes and sizes: there is small pasta, such as vermicelli, for soups, pasta for ravioli and lasagne, pasta shells, extruded pasta like spaghetti and macaroni; noodles which can be thin or wide, white or green, the ribbon-like tagliatelle and the tubular cannelloni.

In this section I will give only the recipes for some of the most common. The range of ready-to-use pasta available in supermarkets is large enough to discourage anyone from making his or her own. But it can be useful to know how to make a basic noodle paste, when you want to try home-made ravioli for instance.

Other dishes made with maize, such as gnocci or polenta, are also included in the pasta section, but rice is not listed here, being used elsewhere with fish, meat, poultry or vegetables, or as a complementary garnish with salad.

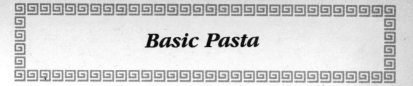

Basic Pasta

Ingredients
225 g/8 oz/2 cups strong plain (bread) flour
225 g/8 oz/1⅓ cups fine semolina (cream of wheat)
5 ml/1 tsp salt
2 whole eggs, beaten
10 ml/2 tsp olive oil
10 ml/2 tsp water

Method
1. Mix the flour, semolina and salt in a bowl. Make a well in the centre and add the beaten egg, oil and water. Blend to a dough and knead for about 8 minutes until it is quite elastic.

2. Roll into a ball and cover with an inverted mixing bowl. Rest for 1 hour.

3. Divide the dough into four pieces. Roll each piece out on a floured board to a thickness of, at most, 3 mm/⅛ in, but the thinner the better. If you are making noodles cut to the width required as stated in the recipe, anything from ½ cm/¼ in to 2 cm/¾ in wide.

4. Separate the noodles and place them on a tray lined with a cloth onto which some semolina has been sprinkled. Leave them to dry for at least 1 hour, but the longer the better. An airing cupboard or hot plate would be quicker. If you do not dry them they will disintegrate on boiling.

<u>Serves 6</u>

Preparation time: 5 mins

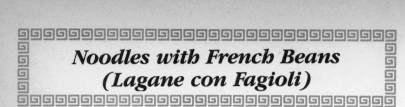

Noodles with French Beans (Lagane con Fagioli)

Ingredients
225 g/8 oz noodles, 1 cm/½ in wide
225 g/8 oz French beans, topped, tailed
and sliced slantwise
50 g/2 oz/¼ cup butter
15 ml/1 tbsp olive oil
1 garlic clove, chopped
Salt and pepper
50 g/2 oz/½ cup grated Parmesan cheese

Method
1. Cook the noodles in boiling salted water in a saucepan for 5 to 8 minutes. Drain.

2. In another pan boil the beans for the same length of time. Drain, refresh in iced water and drain again. This will help to keep the green colour.

3. In a shallow pan heat the butter and oil, stir-fry the garlic for 30 seconds, add the beans and noodles and toss for 3 minutes. Season with salt and black pepper.

4. Serve sprinkled with Parmesan cheese.

<u>Serves 4</u>

Preparation time: 3 mins
Cooking time: 10 mins

Spaghetti with Bacon and Cream (Bucatini alla Carbonara)

Ingredients
225 g/8 oz thin spaghetti
45 ml/3 tbsp olive oil
6 rindless bacon rashers (slices), cut into small strips
2 egg yolks
6 tbsp single (light) cream
50 g/2 oz/½ cup hard cheese, grated
50g/2 oz/¼ cup butter
Salt, pepper and grated nutmeg
Parmesan cheese to serve
25 ml/heaped tbsp chopped (snipped) chives

Method
1. Cook the spaghetti in boiling salted water for approx 12 minutes. Rinse in hot water and drain in a colander.

2. Heat the oil in a pan and stir-fry the bacon strips for 2 minutes, then add the cooked spaghetti.

3. Blend egg yolks, cream and grated cheese in a small bowl.

4. Toss the spaghetti in butter, then in the egg and cream mixture. Season to taste.

5. Serve with extra Parmesan cheese. Sprinkle chives over the pasta.

Serves 4

Preparation time: 5 mins
Cooking time: 11 mins

Green Noodles with Spinach & Tomatoes (Fettucine Verdi al Funghetto)

Ingredients
225 g/8 oz green noodles
225 g/8 oz fresh spinach leaves
45 ml/3 tbsp olive oil
1 garlic clove, chopped
Salt, pepper and grated nutmeg
4 tomatoes, skinned, seeded and chopped
30 ml/2 tbsp butter
50 g/2 oz/½ cup grated Parmesan cheese

Method
1. Cook the noodles for 8 to 10 minutes in boiling salted water. Rinse in hot water and drain in a colander.

2. Wash the spinach leaves, drain and cut the leaves into thin shreds.

3. Heat the oil in a shallow pan and cook the spinach for 2 minutes or more until most of the moisture has evaporated. Add the cooked noodles and garlic. Stir-fry for 2 minutes. Season to taste.

4. Heat the tomatoes with the butter in a pan. Season to taste.

5. Serve the green noodles and spinach coated with the tomato coulis. Serve the grated cheese separately.

<u>*Serves 4*</u>

Preparation time: 5 mins
Cooking time: 12 mins

Thin Noodles with Peppers (Linguine Napoletana)

Ingredients
450 g/1 lb thin noodles
1 red (bell) pepper
60 ml/4 tbsp olive oil
3 garlic cloves
½ fresh chilli (chili)
15 ml/1 tbsp tomato purée (paste)
75 ml/5 tbsp water
Salt and pepper
45 ml/3 tbsp chopped parsley

Method
1. Cook the pasta in boiling salted water for 10 minutes, rinse in hot water and drain in colander.

2. Remove the membrane and seeds from the red pepper and cut in very thin strips, almost like a julienne, 3 mm/⅛ in thick.

3. Heat the oil in a pan and stir-fry the pepper for 3 minutes. Add the garlic, chilli, tomato purée and water. Boil for 3 minutes until the water has evaporated.

4. Toss the linguine in this mixture. Season to taste and sprinkle over fresh parsley. Serve grated cheese (any kind) separately.

Serves 4

Preparation time: 5 mins
Cooking time: 12 mins

Macaroni with Olives and Tuna (Maccheroni Marinara)

Ingredients

225 g/8 oz short cut macaroni
60 ml/4 tbsp olive oil
1 small onion, chopped
1 green chilli (chili), chopped
4 tomatoes, skinned, seeded and chopped
8 black olives, stoned (pitted) and diced
15 ml/1 tbsp pickled capers
200 g/7 oz canned tuna fish, flaked
Salt
45 ml/3 tbsp chopped parsley

Method

1. Cook the macaroni in boiling salted water for 14 minutes. Drain and rinse in hot water.

2. Heat the oil in a pan and stir-fry the onion and chilli for 2 minutes. Add the tomatoes, olives and capers and simmer for 10 minutes. Season to taste.

3. Add the flaked tuna fish and reheat for 2 minutes.

4. Serve macaroni in individual bowls with fish sauce poured over. Sprinkle parsley on top.

Serves 4

Preparation time: 5 mins
Cooking time: 20 mins

Spaghetti with Mushrooms and Prawns (Spaghetti Toscana)

Ingredients
225 g/8 oz spaghetti
60 ml/4 tbsp olive oil
1 garlic clove, chopped
4 strands saffron
1 small onion, chopped
150 g/5 oz/1¼ cups white mushrooms, sliced
150 g/5 oz/1¼ cups peeled cooked prawns (shrimp)
75 ml/6 tbsp dry white wine
5 ml/1 tsp tomato purée (paste)
5 ml/1 tsp cornflour (cornstarch)
45 ml/3 tbsp single (light) cream
Salt and pepper
Fresh parsley, chopped
100 g/4 oz/1 cup grated cheese

Method
1. Cook the spaghetti in boiling salted water for 11 minutes and rinse in hot water. Drain.

2. Heat the oil in a pan and stir-fry the garlic, saffron and onion for 1 minute without browning. Add the mushrooms and prawns. Cook for 2 minutes. Add the wine and tomato purée, boil for 1 minute.

3. Mix the cornflour and cream in a cup and stir this mixture into the main ingredients. Simmer for 3 minutes. Season to taste. Toss the spaghetti in this sauce. Garnish with parsley. Serve cheese separately.

Serves 4

Preparation time: 5 mins
Cooking time: 11 mins

Noodles with Basil and Watercress Sauce (Trenette con Pesto)

Ingredients
225 g/8 oz thin noodles
For the sauce:
45 ml/3 tbsp basil leaves
45 ml/3 tbsp watercress
3 garlic cloves
50 g/2 oz/½ cup grated Sardinian Pecorino cheese
(or Cheddar)
50 g/2 oz/½ cup grated Parmesan cheese
200 ml/7 fl oz/1 scant cup olive oil
Salt and black pepper

Method
1. Cook the noodles in boiling salted water for 10 minutes. Tip into a colander and rinse with hot water.

2. In a mortar, pound the basil, watercress and garlic to a paste. Blend this with the two cheeses and stir in the oil to form an emulsion. (This mixture can also be whirled in a blender for a smoother paste.)

3. Toss the hot noodles in the sauce. Season with salt and black pepper.

Serves 4

Preparation time: 5 mins
Cooking time: 15 mins

Cheesy Macaroni with Chicken (Pastichio con Pollo)

Ingredients
225 g/8 oz short cut macaroni
Salt
50 g/2 oz/¼ cup butter
1 shallot, chopped
225 g/8 oz breast of chicken, without skin, cut into 8 pieces
300 ml/½ pt/1¼ cups Cheese Sauce (see page 22)
Salt, pepper and grated nutmeg
50 g/2 oz/½ cup grated Gruyère cheese
45 ml/3 tbsp chopped parsley

Method
1. Cook the macaroni for 14 minutes in boiling salted water. Rinse in hot water and drain.

2. Heat the butter in a pan and stir-fry the shallot and raw chicken for 5 minutes. Add the cheese sauce and simmer for 4 minutes. Season to taste.

3. Toss the macaroni in this mixture.

4. Place in individual ovenproof dishes, sprinkle with grated cheese and brown in the oven at 200°C/400°F/gas mark 6 for 10 minutes.

5. Serve with parsley sprinkled on top.

Serves 4

Preparation time: 5 mins
Cooking time: 20 mins

Lamb Turnovers with Tomato (Agnolotti con Agnello)

Ingredients
450 g/1 lb Basic Pasta Dough (see page 61)
For the filling:
150 g/5 oz/⅔ cup lean minced (ground) lamb
2 garlic cloves, chopped
60 ml/4 tbsp chopped parsley
1 egg, beaten
30 ml/2 tbsp plain (all-purpose) flour
Salt and black pepper
For the sauce:
300 ml/½ pt/1¼ cups Basquaise Sauce (see page 20)
30 ml/2 tbsp chopped parsley
Grated cheese to serve

Method
1. Roll out the dough on a floured board to a thickness of
3 mm/¼ in into a 25 cm/10 in square. Using a pastry cutter,
make eight rounds 7.5 cm/3 in in diameter. You can use the
trimmings over again.

2. Blend the meat filling ingredients in a bowl and divide the
mixture into eight dumplings. Place each one in the centre of a
pastry round. Wet the edges and fold over to make a semi-
circle. Press the edges tightly. Rest on a tray for 2 hours.

3. Oil a shallow tray and place the ravioli at regular intervals.
Then place in a large pan with enough warm water to cover.
Simmer on top of the stove for 25 minutes. Remove and drain
on a cloth.

4. Place the ravioli on individual flat dishes, two per dish.
Cover with Basquaise sauce and sprinkle parsley on top.

The ravioli pasta will taste better if left covered with the sauce overnight in the refrigerator and reheated when needed.

Serve with grated cheese.

Serves 4

Preparation time: 10 mins
Cooking time: 25 mins

Chapter

5

Seafood Dishes

Seafood Dishes

The markets of the Mediterranean ports look full of colour with their many different and plentiful species of fish including blue tuna, red mullet, brown skate and swordfish. These do, however, have more bones than the better types of fish caught in the North Sea. Sardines are the most popular.

Among the finest and probably dearest are red mullet, whose liver is a delicacy; sea bass a relative of the grouper; John Dory, sea bream and grey mullet which is prized for its roe. The angler fish, known as monkfish, with its ugly head, is also popular; the flesh can be cooked like veal, roasted in butter. The many smaller fish are usually boiled in soups, though lumpfish are also sought after for their eggs.

A favourite in the shell fish section is langouste, known as crawfish and not to be confused with the river crayfish. But most of all in Mediterranean cookery the squid, cuttlefish and octopus dominate the scene. These strange members of the cephalopod family can be fried or stewed and are more tasty than they look.

The recipes listed in this section taste equally good using fish caught in Northern waters such as cod and haddock. But the British market is also generally well stocked with grey mullet and bass as well as all kinds of squids.

It has always been my contention that bones in fish should be removed by the cook rather than leaving it to the consumer. All fishmongers will fillet your fish and clean it if you don't want to do it yourself. Good stocks can be made with bones and fish heads so, if your fishmonger is filleting your fish for you, ask him to include the bits if you intend to make fish soups or sauces. Otherwise don't bother, use a good quality stock cube!

Red Mullet with Garlic and Tomato (Triglie Livornese)

Ingredients
4 red mullet, cleaned and filleted
60 ml/4 tbsp seasoned flour
Oil for shallow frying
1 onion, chopped
1 garlic clove, chopped
3 tomatoes, skinned, seeded and chopped
Salt and pepper
15 ml/1 tbsp tarragon
15 ml/1 tbsp chopped parsley
6 black olives, stoned (pitted)
For the garnish:
100 g/4 oz/½ cup long-grain rice
50 g/2 oz/¼ cup butter
15 ml/1 tbsp turmeric
50 g /2 oz/½ cup grated cheese

Method

1. Roll the fish fillets in seasoned flour. Shake off the surplus.

2. Heat the oil in a pan and fry the fish for 30 seconds only on each side. Transfer the fish to individual flat dishes leaving room for rice garnish.

3. In the same pan stir-fry the onion and garlic for 1 minute then add the chopped tomatoes, tarragon and parsley. Season to taste.

4. Coat the fish with this mixture and dot with black olive pieces. Bake for 5 minutes in a preheated oven at 200°C/ 400°F/gas mark 6 until the fish is almost cooked.

5. Boil the rice for 17 minutes in three times its volume of water. Rinse in hot water. Drain well.

6. In a bowl blend the rice, butter and turmeric. Season to taste.

7. Garnish the fish dish with rice, sprinkle with grated cheese. Bake in the preheated oven for 5 minutes to allow the cheese to brown and to complete the cooking of the fish.

Serves 4

Preparation time: 5 mins
Cooking time: 12 mins

Provençal-style Fish Soup (Bouillabaisse Maison)

It is unlikely that you would get all the Mediterranean fish you need for this dish in one shopping expedition, so this is a simplified version which will taste as good with fewer varieties of fish.

Ingredients
For the stock:
60 ml/4 tbsp olive oil
1 small onion, sliced
1 fennel bulb, chopped
1 garlic clove, chopped
½ small green chilli (chili), seeded and sliced
450 g/1 lb fish bones, washed, rinsed and chopped
1 litre/1¾ pts/4½ cups water
3 strands saffron
15 ml/1 tbsp tomato purée (paste)
Salt and black pepper
For the fish garnish:
1 red fish: red mullet or bream, filleted and skinned
1 white fish: haddock cod or whiting
(Total fish weight: 450 g/1 lb)
4 large frozen tiger prawns (jumbo shrimp)
Salt and black pepper
45 ml/3 tbsp chopped coriander (cilantro) leaves
150 ml/5 fl oz/⅔ cup Aioli Sauce (see page 13)
Garlic bread to serve

Method

1. Heat the oil in a large saucepan and stir-fry the onion, fennel, garlic, chilli and fish bones for 5 minutes.

2. Add the water, saffron and tomato purée and boil for 20 minutes. Strain the liquid into a shallow dish. Season to taste with salt and black pepper.

3. Place the raw fish and prawns in the stock in a shallow dish. Poach for 10 minutes in a preheated oven at 200°C/400°F/gas mark 6.

4. To serve, place the broth and fish in large soup bowls. Sprinkle the coriander on top.

5. Serve the aioli sauce and garlic bread separately.

Serves 4

Preparation time: 10 mins
Cooking time: 15 mins

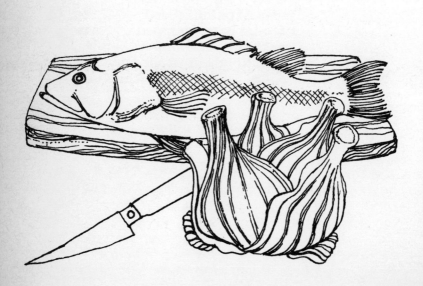

Bass in Fennel Sauce
(Filet de Loup de Mer au Fenouil)

You can make a fish stock by boiling the head and bones of the bass in 2 cups of water for 20 minutes. This will increase the fish flavour, or use a fish stock cube.

Ingredients
45 ml/3 tbsp oil
½ fennel bulb, thinly sliced
150 ml/5 fl oz/⅔ cup white wine
150 ml/5 fl oz/⅔ cup water or fish stock
7.5 ml/½ tbsp flour and 7.5 ml/½ tbsp butter
blended to a paste
Salt and black pepper
2 bass fillets, with skins, weighing about 225 g/8 oz each

Method
1. Heat the oil in a pan and stir-fry the fennel for 2 minutes. Add the wine and stock and boil for 8 minutes. Add the butter and flour paste and whisk to obtain a smooth mixture. Season to taste.

2. Transfer this sauce into a shallow earthenware dish. Place the fish fillets on top and season to taste.

3. Bake in a preheated oven at 200°C/400°F/gas mark 6 for 15 minutes, basting the fish from time to time. Serve from the dish.

<u>Serves 2</u>

Preparation time: 5 mins
Cooking time: 12 mins

Sweet and Sour Fried Fish
(Pescado Escabeche)

Ingredients
450 g/1 lb mackerel, filleted
60 ml/4 tbsp seasoned flour
60 ml/4 tbsp oil
For the sauce:
2 tomatoes, skinned, seeded and chopped
2.5 ml/½ tsp curry powder
5 ml/1 tsp green chilli (chili), seeded and chopped
300 ml/½ pt/1¼ cups water
Grated rind and juice of ½ an orange and 1 lemon
Salt and pepper
Pinch of ground cumin
45 ml/3 tbsp olive oil
45 ml/3 tbsp vinegar
30 ml/2 tbsp sugar
30 ml/2 tbsp chopped parsley or coriander (cilantro)

Method

1. Clean and wash the fish and pat dry. Dip in seasoned flour and shake off any surplus.

2. Heat the oil in a frying pan (skillet) and cook the mackerel for
3 minutes on each side. Transfer to a shallow dish.

3. Boil the sauce ingredients for 4 minutes and pour over the fish. Cool and chill for 2 hours.
Sprinkle parsley over when serving.

This preparation applies to any kind of fried fish.

Serves 4

Preparation time: 5 mins
Cooking time: 5 mins

Monk Fish with Garlic
(Lotte Rôtie Riviera)

Only the tail of this angler fish is used. The skin can be removed either before roasting or after.

Ingredients
1 kg/2¼ lb piece of monk fish
6 garlic cloves, cut in small slivers
50 g/2 oz/¼ cup butter and oil mixed
Salt and pepper
225 g/8 oz potatoes, peeled and sliced
120 ml/4 fl oz/½ cup single (light) cream
45 ml/3 tbsp chopped parsley

Method
1. Wash the fish and pat dry. Make a little cut with the point of a knife and insert slivers of garlic as you would do for a leg of lamb.

2. Brush with butter and oil. Season to taste. Bake in a preheated oven at 200°C/400°F/gas mark 6 for 20 minutes, basting from time to time and turning the fish over after 10 minutes.

3. While the fish is cooking, boil the sliced potatoes for 8 minutes. When cooked, drain off the liquid and mash with the seasoning and cream.

4. When ready, remove the tail, discard the skin and fillet the fish. Cut into four portions and serve with creamed potatoes. Sprinkle parsley over the fish and potatoes.

Serves 4

Preparation time: 5 mins
Cooking time: 20 mins

Dublin Bay Prawns with Pepper and Tomato Sauce (Scamponi Sorrentina)

Ingredients
For the sauce:
45 ml/3 tbsp oil
1 red (bell) pepper, seeded and cut into fine strips
3 garlic cloves, chopped
2 large tomatoes, skinned, seeded and chopped
10 ml/2 tsp fresh or 5 ml/1 tsp dried tarragon, chopped
5 ml/1 tsp chopped parsley
Salt and pepper
120 ml/4 fl oz/½ cup single (light) cream
For the prawns (shrimp):
1 kg/2¼ lb king prawns (jumbo shrimp) in their shells, fresh or frozen
45 ml/3 tbsp seasoned flour
Oil for shallow-frying
225 g/8 oz/1 cup long grain rice

Method
1. Heat the oil in a wok or pan and stir-fry the red peppers for 2 minutes, add the garlic and cook for 30 seconds.

2. Blend in the tomatoes and herbs. Season to taste. Cook for 2 minutes and add the cream.

3. Remove the prawn shells without breaking the flesh. Cut off the intestinal tube near the tail end, wash, pat dry and dip in seasoned flour.

4. Heat the oil in a wok or pan and fry the prawns for 3 minutes. Drain well.

5. Stir the cooked prawns into the sauce and spoon onto plates. Serve with long grain rice boiled for 20 minutes, rinsed in hot water and dried in a preheated oven at 190°C/375°F/ gas mark 5 for 10 minutes.

Small lobsters can be cooked in the same way, but are best left in the shell, boiled for 2 minutes then shelled and reheated in the sauce.

Serves 4

Preparation time: 10 mins
Cooking time: 5 mins

Fried Sardines with Lemon Sauce (Sarde in Salsa)

The bones of small sardines are edible but larger ones need to be filleted. Pilchards and small herrings with the bones removed could equally well be used.

Ingredients
16 sardines, filleted, cleaned and dried
60 ml/4 tbsp seasoned flour
1 egg, beaten
100 g/4 oz/1 cup plain (all-purpose) flour
300 ml/½ pt/1¼ cups milk
Salt
Oil for shallow-frying
For the lemon sauce:
Juice and grated rind of 1 lemon
120 ml/4 fl oz/½ cup natural (plain) yoghurt
Salt and pepper
15 ml/1 tbsp sugar
15 ml/1 tbsp chopped parsley

Method
1. Dip the fillets in seasoned flour and shake off the surplus.

2. Make a batter by blending the egg, flour, milk and seasoning.

3. Dip the fish fillets in batter, drain and shallow-fry in hot oil for
1 minute until golden. Drain on absorbent paper.

4. Mix the sauce ingredients in a bowl and serve with
the fried sardines.

Serves 4

Preparation time: 5 mins
Cooking time: 4 mins

Fresh Tuna Fish in a Piquante Sauce (Tonno Calabrese)

Fresh tuna fish is now appearing on the fishmonger's slab and this recipe provides an excellent opportunity to use it.

Ingredients
4 tuna steaks on the bone, each 200 g/7 oz
60 ml/4 tbsp seasoned flour
For the sauce:
60 ml/4 tbsp olive oil
2 garlic cloves, chopped
1 spring onion (scallion), chopped
45 ml/3 tbsp wine vinegar
15 ml/1 tbsp pickled capers
15 ml/1 tbsp gherkins, chopped
5 ml/1 tsp made mustard
30 ml/2 tbsp single (light) cream
Salt and pepper
5 ml/1 tsp sugar
30 ml/2 tbsp chopped parsley

Method
1. Wash and dry the tuna fish steaks. Then dip in seasoned flour.

2. Heat the oil in a shallow pan and fry (sauté) for 3 minutes on both sides.

3. While the fish is cooking, make the sauce by blending all the ingredients in a bowl, whisking the mixture slightly.

4. When fish is cooked, discard central bone and serve on plates with piquante sauce and a tomato or green salad.

Serves 2

Preparation time: 5 mins
Cooking time: 4 mins

Sea Food Kebab
(Brochette Provençale)

Ingredients
4 scallops
4 pieces of monk fish, or other firm fish,
cut into 4 cm/1½ in cubes
8 tiger prawns (jumbo shrimp), shelled
1 bulb fennel cut into 4 cm/1½ in squares
1 red (bell) pepper, seeded and cut
into 4 cm/1½ in squares
8 white mushroom caps
1 onion, cut into 4 and divided into layers
4 bay leaves
For the marinade:
60 ml/4 tbsp olive oil
Juice of ½ lemon
1 garlic clove, chopped
Salt and pepper

Method
1. Clean the scallops and use the white flesh and coral. Fillet the white fish and cut into cubes.

2. In a bowl, marinate all the ingredients for 1 hour. Spear the ingredients on a 20 cm/8 in long kebab in this order per portion: 1 square of red pepper, 1 scallop, 1 mushroom, 1 bay leaf, 1 fish, 1 fennel, 1 prawn, and 1 piece of onion, alternating peppers, mushrooms, onion and fennel between each seafood item.
Fill four kebabs.

3. Brush with oil marinade and grill for 8 minutes.
Serve with mixed salad.

Serves 2

Preparation time: 5 mins
Cooking time: 6 mins

Chapter

6

Beef and Veal Dishes

Beef and Veal Dishes

Veal, rather more than beef, seems to be the more popular meat in the southern European countries, although beef is becoming more popular and minced meats have always been used. A traditional Bolognese sauce is a complex and long-cooked dish involving a long list of ingredients. We are familiar with a simpler version which finds its way into many dishes as stuffing for courgettes, aubergines, onions and tomatoes. The French Carmargue is well known for its cattle and the Chianini steers of Tuscany have a wide reputation. Yet Italy, Provençal France and Spain are not known as roast beef countries.

It is a fact that most western Mediterranean countries, including all the islands, eat more pork than beef and more lamb than veal. So in this section you will find familiar beef and veal dishes made up of the quintessence of Mediterranean cuisine with herbs and wines being used to enhance the flavour.

Beef with Spinach and Mushrooms (Pignatella di Bue)

Ingredients
225 g/8 oz fillet of beef or veal
30 ml/2 tbsp vermouth
5 ml/1 tsp honey
60 ml/4 tbsp olive oil
225 g/8 oz spinach
1 garlic clove, chopped
2 white mushrooms, sliced
75 ml/5 tbsp water
1 beef stock cube
2.5 ml/½ tsp cornflour (cornstarch)
Salt and black pepper
Ground ginger

Method
1. Remove the skin and fat from the fillet. Cut into 5 mm/¼ in slices, then in strips. Soak in a bowl with vermouth, honey and 15 ml/1 tbsp of the olive oil. Cover with a lid and refrigerate for 2 hours.

2. Wash the spinach, remove the stems. Drain and pat dry. Cut the stems into 2.5 cm/1 in slices and shred the large leaves.

3. Heat 30 ml/2 tbsp of the oil in a large shallow frying pan (skillet). Brown the meat slices for 2 minutes. Remove from the pan. Add the spinach, garlic, marinade, mushrooms, water, stock cube and cornflour.

4. Stir until the mixture begins to boil then add the spinach leaves and stems. Stir over high heat for 3 to 4 minutes until the spinach and meat are cooked.
Season and serve with thin noodles.

Serves 2

Preparation time: 10 mins
Cooking time: 5 mins

Braised Beef in Wine
(Boeuf à la Mode Antiboise)

Ingredients
60 ml/4 tbsp oil
1 joint of beef, 2.25 kg/5 lb
from topside, thick flank, oven ready
2 calves' feet, split
1 bottle red Provençal wine
2 carrots, cubed
2 onions, chopped
2 celery sticks (ribs), diced
30 ml/2 tbsp tomato purée (paste)
4 garlic cloves, chopped
1 sprig of thyme
250 ml/8 fl oz/1 cup water
15 ml/1 tbsp cornflour (cornstarch)
mixed with 45 ml/3 tbsp water
Salt and black pepper

Method
1. Heat the oil in a pan and fry (sauté) the joint all over to brown the outside of the meat for 4 minutes.

2. Place the calves' feet in a deep casserole dish (Dutch oven) with the joint on top.

3. Stir-fry the vegetables in the pan for 2 minutes and add to the casserole with the tomato purée, garlic, thyme and wine.

4. Cover with a lid and braise in a preheated oven at 180°C/ 350°F/gas mark 4 for 2 hours. After one hour add 1 cup of water and turn the joint over.

5. When done, remove the joint and strings. Carve in thick portions. Strain the sauce through a colander and discard calves' feet bones. Dice the flesh and serve it as a garnish, or elsewhere as an hors d'oeuvre.

6. Pour gravy into a saucepan. The vegetables can be saved and used in soup. Remove any surplus fat on top of gravy. Season to taste and bring to the boil.

7. Use the blended cornflour and water to thicken the gravy. Boil for a further 4 minutes and strain. All vegetables and calves' feet meat can be used elsewhere. Fresh vegetables are cooked separately to accompany the dish.

Serves 8

Preparation time: 10 mins
Cooking time: 2 hours

Provençal Casserole
(Casserole Provençal)

Ingredients
900 g/2 lb lean beef, cubed
100 g/4 oz/scant 1 cup belly pork, rinded and cubed
1 onion, chopped
5 ml/1 tsp mixed herbs
Salt and pepper
250 ml/8 fl oz/1 cup dry red wine
30 ml/2 tbsp plain (all-purpose) flour
30 ml/2 tbsp olive oil
2 garlic cloves, chopped
1 green (bell) pepper, chopped
60 ml/4 tbsp water
5 ml/1 tsp paprika
1 bouquet garni
8 black olives, stoned (pitted)

Method

1. Put the beef, pork, onion, herbs, salt and pepper and red wine in a dish, cover and leave to marinate overnight.

2. Remove the meat and pat it dry. Season the flour with salt and pepper then toss the meat in the flour.

3. Heat the oil in a flameproof casserole (Dutch oven) and fry (sauté) the meat until browned.

4. Add the garlic and pepper and fry for 2 minutes.

5. Stir in all the remaining ingredients except the olives and bring to the boil. Transfer to a preheated oven and cook at 140°C/275°F/gas mark 1 for 4 hours.

6. Remove the boquet garni and leave the casserole to cool so that any fat rises to the surface. Skim off the fat.

7. When ready to serve, skim off the fat, reheat the dish and stir in the olives. Serve with chunks of crusty bread.

Serves 4

Preparation time: 10 mins
Cooking time: 4½ hours plus marinating

Beef Fillet with Pepper and Celery (Pepperoni di Bue)

Ingredients
1 red (bell) pepper
1 celery stick (rib)
1 onion
60 ml/4 tbsp oil
2 fillet steaks, trimmed and cut into thin strips
1 garlic clove
1.5 ml/¼ tsp mixed spice
120 ml/4 fl oz/½ cup red wine
5 ml/1 tsp cornflour (cornstarch)
1 beef stock cube
Salt and pepper
Boiled rice to serve

Method
1. Seed and slice the red pepper into thin strips. Cut the celery into same size strips. Cut the onion in four and divide into layers. Slice each layer into strips.

2. Heat the oil in a large frying pan (skillet) and stir-fry the meat strips with garlic and spices until brown. Add the red pepper, celery and onion and fry for a further 2 minutes.

3. Stir the wine and cornflour together in a cup and add to the mixture. Boil and add the crumbled stock cube. Stir until the sauce thickens to a glossy consistency. Season with salt and pepper. Serve with plain boiled rice.

Serves 2

Preparation time: 5 mins
Cooking time: 10 mins

Veal with Caper Sauce
(Vitello di Bue Capperi)

Use thin flank steaks well hammered, lean chuck steaks or veal.

Ingredients
2 veal steaks, 225 g/8 oz each, free of fat and gristle
Salt and black pepper
60 ml/4 tbsp oil
For the sauce:
25 g/1 oz/2 tbsp butter
15 ml/1 tbsp small pickled capers
1 small gherkin, chopped
45 ml/3 tbsp wine vinegar
5 ml/1 tsp honey
5 ml/1 tsp tomato purée (paste) or ketchup (catsup)
Salt and black pepper
15 ml/1 tbsp chopped parsley and tarragon

Method
1. Beat the veal to a thickness of 5 mm/¼ in. Brush with oil.

2. Heat the oil in the pan and quickly sauté the veal for 1 minute on each side. Season to taste and remove from the pan. Put on two hot plates.

3. Combine all the sauce ingredients in a bowl, except the butter and herbs.

4. In the same pan boil the sauce ingredients for 2 minutes. Add the soft butter and whisk to obtain an emulsion. Pour this sauce over each veal steak. Sprinkle with fresh herbs. Serve with grilled tomatoes and mushrooms.

Serves 2

Preparation time: 5 mins
Cooking time: 5 mins

Veal Escalope with Spaghetti (Scaloppe di Vitello Milanese)

This is probably the best known way of cooking veal outside of the Mediterranean countries. To achieve the perfect escalope you need to beat it gently with a wooden mallet. Wet or oil the escalope, place it between two polythene sheets, and gently beat it to double the surface of the meat to a thickness of 5 mm/¼ in. This is not done to make the escalope more tender, but to make it larger.

Ingredients
225 g/8 oz veal from loin or thick part of leg
Salt and black pepper
30 ml/2 tbsp seasoned flour
1 egg, beaten with 45 ml/3 tbsp water or milk
100 g/4 oz/2 cups breadcrumbs
60 ml/4 tbsp oil for frying
50 g/2 oz/¼ cup butter
Juice of ½ lemon
2 slices of lemon
15 ml/1 tbsp chopped parsley
225 g/8 oz of spaghetti, cooked in
Fresh Tomato Sauce (see page 19)

Method
1. Cut veal into two slices and beat each slice with a wooden mallet to achieve an area of 8 cm/3¼ in by 24 cm/9½ in and 5 mm/¼ in thick. Season with salt and black pepper. Toss in flour, dust off surplus, dip in beaten egg then in breadcrumbs.

2. Heat the oil and cook for 1½ minutes on each side.

3. Heat the butter until it froths and pour over the cooked escalopes. Squeeze a little lemon juice over the veal and serve with a slice of lemon. Sprinkle with parsley.

4. Serve with cooked spaghetti in tomato sauce or
any other vegetables.

Serves 2

Preparation time: 8 mins
Cooking time: 6 mins

Veal with Marsala (Vitello Marsala)

Ingredients
**2 thin escalopes, 150 g/5 oz each cut into two pieces,
beaten as in previous recipe
30 ml/2 tbsp seasoned flour
30 ml/2 tbsp butter and oil
75 ml/5 tbsp dry Marsala
45 ml/3 tbsp single (light) cream
Salt and pepper**

Method
1. Dip the escalopes in flour and dust off the surplus. Heat the
mixture of butter and oil in a pan. Cook the escalopes for
1½ minutes on each side until golden.

2. Remove some of the surplus fat, add the marsala and boil
for 30 seconds, then add the cream. Simmer the meat for
1 minute only. Season to taste. Serve with the sauce.

Serves 2

Preparation time: 5 mins
Cooking time: 5 mins

Calves' Liver in Peppercorn Sauce (Foie de Veau au Poivre Vert)

Ingredients
225 g/8 oz calves' liver, cut into 2 slices
Seasoned flour
60 ml/4 tbsp oil
For the sauce:
1 small onion
5 ml/1 tsp tomato purée (paste)
5 ml/1 tsp meat extract
120 ml/4 fl oz/½ cup water or wine
5 ml/1 tsp pickled green peppercorns
60 ml/4 tbsp double (heavy) cream
Salt
For the garnish:
225 g/8 oz baby carrots
5 ml/1 tsp honey
30 ml/2 tbsp butter
Salt
Fresh mint leaves, chopped

Method
1. Wash the liver and drain. Pat dry and rub with a little flour.

2. Heat the oil in a shallow pan and fry the liver for 4 minutes. Remove from the pan and keep hot.

3. In the same pan fry the onion for 1 minute, add the tomato purée, meat extract and water or wine and boil for 5 minutes.

4. Strain the sauce into a small saucepan. Add the peppercorns and reboil. Stir in the cream and simmer for a further 2 minutes. Season with salt to taste.

5. Wash the baby carrots and drain. Boil the carrots just covered with water, add the honey, butter, and season with salt to taste. Cook for 8 minutes until the liquid is almost evaporated. The carrots should be firm and crunchy.

6. Pour a pool of the sauce on plates, add the liver and garnish with carrots. Sprinkle with chopped mint and serve hot.

Serves 2

Preparation time: 5 mins
Cooking time: 5 mins

Veal and Ham Kebab (Oseleti Scampai)

Ingredients
1 slice of calves' liver, cubed
1 veal escalope, cubed
4 rindless bacon rashers (slices)
8 button onions
8 small mushroom caps
Fresh sage leaves
60 ml/4 tbsp oil for cooking
Salt and black pepper

Method
1. Cut the meats into 3 cm/1¼ in squares. On kebab skewers, at least 20 cm/8 in long, spear the liver, veal and bacon pieces alternately between onions, mushrooms and fresh sage leaves.

2. Brush with oil and season with salt and black pepper. Grill (broil) for 8 to 10 minutes, brushing with oil from time to time.

Serves 2

Preparation time: 5 mins
Cooking time: 8-10 mins

Calves' Kidneys in Wine Sauce (Rogonnade)

Ingredients
2 calves' kidneys, all skin, fat and sinews removed
Seasoned flour
60 ml/4 tbsp oil and butter
1 shallot, chopped
150 ml/5 fl oz/⅔ cup dry Vermouth or Madeira wine
Pinch dried tarragon
2.5 ml/½ tsp meat extract or marmite
120 ml/4 fl oz/½ cup single (light) cream
Salt and black pepper
5 ml/1 tsp Dijon mustard
30 ml/2 tbsp chopped parsley

Method
1. Slice the kidney thinly, dip the slices in seasoned flour and shake off the surplus.

2. Heat the oil and butter in a wok or large frying pan (skillet). Stir-fry the kidneys for 4 minutes then add the shallot and cook for 1 more minute. Remove from the pan and keep hot while finishing the sauce.

3. Remove the surplus fat and in the same pan boil the wine for 2 minutes. Add the tarragon, meat extract or marmite and cream. Boil for a further 2 minutes. Reheat the cooked kidneys in this delicious sauce without boiling. Season to taste. Lastly add the mustard and sprinkle with parsley. Serve as a light entrée on its own.

Serves 4

Preparation time: 5 mins
Cooking time: 8 mins

Veal Escalope with Ham and Cheese (Vitello Saltimbocca)

Saltimbocca means 'melt in the mouth'. This refers to the cheese which is sandwiched between veal and ham. Many people believe that prosciutto is a specific name for the delicate salmon coloured Parma ham which often accompanies melon. Actually the Italian word simply means any kind of ham, fresh or cured. So in this dish you can use any ham and veal produced in your own country.

Ingredients
2 veal escalopes, each weighing 150 g/5 oz, beaten very thin
1 egg, beaten
2 thin slices of ham, half the size of the veal
2 thin slices of Mozzarella or processed cheese,
same size as the ham
Seasoned flour
Breadcrumbs
60 ml/4 tbsp oil for cooking

Method
1. Brush the veal escalopes with egg. Place a slice of ham and a slice of cheese on top of each other on one side of the veal escalope. Fold over to envelop the cheese and ham.

2. Dip the escalope in flour, then in beaten egg, then in breadcrumbs. Heat the oil and fry (sauté) for 2 minutes on each side. Drain well and serve with a green or tomato salad.

Serves 2

Preparation time: 8 mins
Cooking time: 8 mins

Chapter
7
Lamb Dishes

Lamb Dishes

Lamb has a symbolic significance in all Latin countries. It is partly because of religious traditions that the Mediterranean people have a reverence as much as a liking for sheep. That does not mean they produce better quality animals than in Great Britain. The pastures of the highlands of Wales and Scotland provide the best fodder for lamb, hence its superior quality. Some gourmet said once that lamb requires no more cooking than bread. It must be pure and should not need garlic, rosemary or other spices. Roast or grilled, lamb is the perfect meat which, when cooked for the right length of time, is mouthwateringly succulent.

The Latins have condemned the practice of serving mint sauce or redcurrant jelly with roast lamb, while contrarily they destroy the natural taste by adding far too much garlic and the stronger herbs. British readers will know that it makes sense to leave good things well alone. A sauce is a good sauce when it does not camouflage the real flavour of the main ingredients.

Each region has its own favourite way of cooking lamb but in this section we shall explore lamb dishes that have the flavour of rosemary mingling with other aromatic herbs of Provence. You will find that the British supermarkets are well stocked with different cuts of lamb, from boneless joints to prepared kebabs, as well as minced and diced lamb for pies which, in the long run, will save time in preparation.

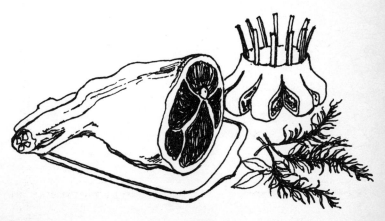

Greek Lamb Kebab with Feta Cheese (Souvlakia)

Ingredients
4 boneless lamb chops
Feta cheese, cut into 2.5 cm/1 in cubes
1 red (bell) pepper, seeded and
cut into 3 cm/1¼ in square pieces
12 large olives, stoned (pitted)
1 fennel bulb, cut in 3 cm/1¼ in squares
12 button onions
1 garlic clove, chopped
For the marinade:
150 ml/5 fl oz/⅔ cup dry white wine
45 ml/3 tbsp olive oil
Juice and grated rind of 1 lemon
Salt and pepper

Method
1. Cut each chop into 4 small pieces.

2. In a bowl assemble all the ingredients of the marinade. Soak the lamb and feta cheese cubes for 2 hours.

3. On two long kebab skewers spear the meat alternately with the pepper, olives, fennel, onions, garlic and feta cubes.

4. Brush marinade over and grill (broil) for 3 minutes on each side, basting all the time.

5. Prepare a lamb gravy (see page 108) and add the remaining marinade liquid and reboil for 2 minutes. Serve with plain rice or boiled new potatoes.

Serves 2

Preparation time: 8 mins
Cooking time: 7 mins

Lamb with Quince
(Agneau aux Coings)

Ingredients
30 ml/2 tbsp olive oil
2 onions, chopped
450 g/1 lb lean lamb, cubed
225 g/8 oz tomatoes, skinned and roughly chopped
7.5 ml/1½ tsp cinnamon
Salt and pepper
450 g/1 lb quinces or firm apples

Method
1. Heat the oil and fry (sauté) the onions until soft. Add the lamb and fry until lightly browned on all sides.

2. Just cover the meat with water and add the tomatoes and cinnamon. Season with salt and pepper.

3. Bring to the boil, cover and simmer gently for about 45 minutes until the meat is tender, stirring occasionally and adding a little more water during cooking if necessary.

4. Meanwhile, core the quinces and cut them into halves or quarters depending on the size. Add to the pan, cover and simmer for about 15 minutes until the quinces are soft, again adding a little more water if the dish appears too dry. Serve with rice.

Serves 4

Preparation time: 8 mins
Cooking time: 1 hour

Greek-style Lamb Stew (Agnello di Lemone)

Ingredients
60 ml/4 tbsp olive oil
450 g/1 lb lamb, cut in 2.5 cm/1 in cubes
100 g/4 oz celery sticks (ribs), diced
2 parsnips, diced
1 onion, chopped
1 garlic clove, chopped
600 ml/1 pt/2½ cups water
2.5 ml/½ tsp coriander (cilantro) seeds
12 button mushrooms, caps only
For the sauce:
15 ml/1 tbsp plain (all-purpose) flour
7.5 ml/½ tbsp cornflour (cornstarch)
3 egg yolks
Salt and pepper
Juice and grated rind of 1 lemon
15 ml/1 tbsp honey
30 ml/2 tbsp lemon grass, chopped
3 mint leaves, chopped

Method
1. Heat the oil in a flameproof casserole dish (Dutch oven). Stir-fry the lamb for 4 minutes. Add the celery, parsnips, onion and garlic. Cook for a further 2 minutes without browning.

2. Add the water and coriander seeds. Bring to the boil and simmer gently. Remove scum as it rises. Cover with a lid and lower the heat. Add hot water to keep the level up during cooking. After 1½ hours add the mushrooms.

3. In a bowl mix the flour and cornflour with the egg yolks. Using a whisk grandually add 1 cup of the meat stock to this mixture. Check that the meat is almost ready and, if so, transfer the egg mixture into the boiling stew and let it bubble away for a further 4 minutes, stirring. Season to taste. Add the grated rind, lemon juice and honey.

4. Serve in soup plates with a generous sprinkling of lemon grass and mint leaves. Boiled rice or potatoes make a good accompaniment.

Serves 4

Preparation time: 5 mins
Cooking time: 1½ hours

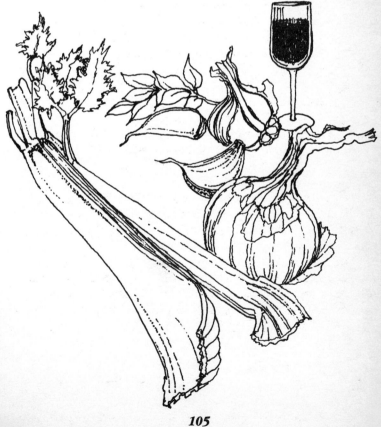

Minced Lamb Pie
(Gâteau d'Agneau Pascaline)

Ingredients
225 g/8 oz shortcrust pastry (basic pie crust)
1 egg yolk
For the filling:
225 g/8 oz/1 cup minced (ground) lean lamb
1 shallot, chopped
30 ml/2 tbsp chopped parsley
1 egg, beaten
75 ml/5 tbsp brandy
50 g/2 oz/1 cup white breadcrumbs
45 ml/3 tbsp single (light) cream
Salt and pepper
For the topping:
1 potato, peeled and thinly sliced
50 g/2 oz/¼ cup butter

Method
1. Oil a metal flan tin and line it with shortcrust pastry 5 mm/¼ in thick. Prick the bottom of the pastry and brush it with egg yolk.

2. In a bowl, blend the minced lamb with the shallot, parsley, beaten egg, brandy, breadcrumbs and cream. Add seasoning.

3. Fill the pastry case with a layer of the meat and cover with thin slices of potato overlapping each other.
Brush the top with plenty of butter.

4. Bake in a preheated oven at 200°C/400°F/gas mark 6 on the top shelf for 45 minutes, brushing the top with butter from time to time. When brown, cover with greased foil to prevent potatoes from drying and burning.

5. Serve hot with a green salad in garlic dressing.

Serves 4

Preparation time: 8 mins
Cooking time: 45 mins

Lamb's Liver with Apricots (Foie d'Agneau Abricotine)

If you prefer your liver slightly bleached, soak it in salted water for 1 hour. Dry it, then soak in a little milk for 10 minutes. Pat dry.

Ingredients
4 thin slices of lamb's liver, 225 g/8 oz per portion
Seasoned flour
2 eggs, beaten
100 g/4 oz/1½ cups mixture of breadcrumbs and sesame seeds
Oil for shallow frying
4 fresh apricots, stoned
30 ml/2 tbsp honey

Method
1. Rub the liver in seasoned flour. Shake off the surplus and dip in beaten eggs then in crumb and seed mixture.

2. Heat the oil in a pan and quickly fry on both sides for 1 minute only. Remove and place in a flat earthenware dish. Arrange one halved apricot on each slice of fried liver. Brush with hot honey and brown under the grill (broiler) to soften the apricots.

3. Serve with a curly green salad.

Serves 2

Preparation time: 5 mins
Cooking time: 5 mins

Roast Rack of Lamb
(Carré d'Agneau Antiboise)

Ingredients
1 rack of lamb with 7 ribs, trimmed.
The ribs will be no more than 10 cm/4 in in length
and the fat covering the ribs must be removed to
within 2.5 cm/1 in of the eye muscle. The rib fingers
will be removed to expose approximately 2 cm/¾ in of
the rib bones, and spine bone must be removed.
1 egg, beaten
15 ml/1 tbsp nibbed almonds
60 ml/4 tbsp breadcrumbs
2.5 ml/½ tsp each of dried rosemary, thyme, sage and basil
Salt and black pepper
30 ml/2 tbsp oil
For the lamb gravy:
250 g/9 oz lamb bones
1 small onion, sliced
1 carrot, sliced
1 celery stick (rib), chopped
300 ml/½ pt/1¼ cup water
1 beef stock cube
1 garlic clove, chopped
Salt and pepper
45 ml/3 tbsp medium sherry
7.5 ml/½ tbsp cornflour (cornstarch) (optional)

Method
1. To make the lamb gravy, brown the bones in a hot oven
half-an-hour before cooking the rack. Remove when brown.
Place the bones, onion, carrot and celery in a saucepan with the
water, beef stock cube and raw garlic. Boil to reduce it by half.
Season to taste. Remove surplus fat and add the medium sherry.

2. This gravy can be slightly thickened with 7.5 ml/½ tbsp cornflour
diluted in the sherry and added to the sauce after the gravy has
boiled for 12 minutes. Season to taste. Strain and keep warm.

3. Take the rack of lamb and make sure the skin has been peeled off, exposing the fat. Make a criss-cross pattern in the fat with the point of a knife. Brush with beaten egg.

4. Combine the almonds, breadcrumbs and herbs in a bowl with salt and pepper. Press the fat side of the rack onto the crumbs to make them stick as a coating. Splash a little oil over the crumb side of the rack.

5. Preheat the oven to 230°C/450°F/gas mark 8. Place the rack of lamb in a metal tin (pan) and roast for 15 minutes. Turn the rack over when golden brown, basting with oil to prevent burning. The meat should be juicy and slightly pink.

6. Carve by cutting between ribs. The last rib bone is discarded. Serve with sauté potatoes and the lamb gravy.

Serves 2

Preparation time: 8 mins
Cooking time: 25 to 30 mins

Lamb Cubes Sautéd Sicilian-style (Ragu al Capone)

Ingredients
60 ml/4 tbsp olive oil
8 lamb cutlets, with bone removed
1 green chilli (chili), sliced
1 onion, cut in four with layers separated
1 red (bell) pepper, seeded and cut into 2.5 cm/1 in squares
3 celery sticks (ribs), cut slantwise 1 cm/½ in thick
12 button mushrooms
1 garlic clove, chopped
5 ml/1 tsp tomato purée (paste)
120 ml/4 fl oz/½ cup medium sherry
15 ml/1 tbsp cornflour (cornstarch)
45 ml/3 tbsp water
Salt and black pepper

Method
1. Remove the fat, using only the lean meat.

2. Heat the oil in a large frying pan (skillet). Add the meat and brown all over for 4 minutes. Remove from the pan and keep warm.

3. In the same pan, using the same oil, stir-fry the onion, pepper, celery and mushrooms for 1 minute. Add the garlic, chilli, lamb, tomato purée and sherry. Bring to the boil and add the blended cornflour and water to thicken mixture. Season. Cook for a further 2 minutes.

4. Serve with rice or noodles.

Serves 4

Preparation time: 10 mins
Cooking time: 8 mins

Baked Lamb Cutlets
(Costolettine di Agnello Calabrese)

Ingredients
1 large aubergine (eggplant), sliced
Salt
60 ml/4 tbsp oil for frying
2 large potatoes, sliced
1 large onion, sliced
2 courgettes (zucchini), sliced
4 large tomatoes, skinned, seeded and cut in slices
300 ml/½ pt/1¼ cups Chianti wine
3 garlic cloves, chopped
8 middle lamb cutlets, trimmed
225 g/8 oz Mozarella cheese, sliced
6 basil leaves, chopped

Method
1. Soak the aubergine slices in salted water for 15 minutes. Rinse and pat dry. In a pan heat 30 ml/2 tbsp of oil and fry (sauté) the aubergine slices for 30 seconds. Remove and drain. In the same oil stir-fry the onion for 2 minutes.

2. In a deep earthernware dish arrange a row of sliced potatoes and top it with a layer of onion, raw courgettes and tomatoes. Add red wine and garlic.

3. Fry the cutlets in the pan for 1 minute on each side to brown them. Season and place the cutlets on the vegetables in the dish. Cover with fried aubergines and slices of mozzarella. Bake in a preheated oven at 200°C/400°F/gas mark 6 for 45 minutes.

4. Serve sprinkled with chopped basil.

Serves 4

Preparation time: 8 mins
Cooking time: 45 mins

Roast Leg of Lamb with Rosemary (Gigot d'Agneau Rôti Maltaise)

Ingredients
1.5 kg/3 lb boned leg of lamb
3 garlic cloves, cut into small slivers
1 lemon, cut in half
A few sprigs of rosemary
45 ml/3 tbsp butter and oil
Salt and black pepper
Lamb bones
1 carrot, cut in chunks
1 onion, quartered
1 celery stick (rib), chopped roughly
300 ml/½ pt/1¼ cups water
300 ml/½ pt/1¼ cups juice of sweet blood oranges
and grated rind of 1 orange
5 ml/1 tsp ground ginger
15 ml/1 tbsp cornflour (cornstarch) (optional)
15 ml/1 tbsp redcurrant jelly (clear conserve)

Method
1. Make incisions around the outside of the leg and insert slivers of garlic. Rub the lamb with halved lemon and push a sprig of rosemary inside the bone cavity. Brush with butter and oil, and season with salt and black pepper.

2. Put the lamb on a trivet of bones in a roasting tin (baking pan). Add the water and roast in a preheated oven 200°C/400°F/gas mark 6 for 1 hour. Reduce the heat to 190°C/375°F/gas mark 5 for the remaining half hour. Baste from time to time with the water. Add the carrot, onion and celery half an hour before
the meat is cooked.

3. When the meat is cooked place it in a deep serving dish and keep hot while making the gravy.

4. Remove most of the fat from the roasting tin, but leave the meat juice, carrot, celery and bone. Add the rosemary, orange rind, orange juice and ginger and boil rapidly for 10 minutes.

5. Season to taste. If thickening, blend the cornflour with 45 ml/3 tbsp of water, add to gravy and cook for 3 minutes. Strain. Finally, stir the redcurrant jelly into the gravy.

Serves 8

Preparation time: 12 mins
Cooking time: 1¼ hours

Mediterranean Lamb Casserole
(Haricot d'Agneau Méditerranée)

Ingredients
100 g/4 oz/⅔ cup haricot beans, soaked overnight
750 g/1½ lb stewing lamb from shoulder
Seasoned flour
75 ml/5 tbsp oil
1 onion, chopped
3 garlic cloves, chopped
300 ml/½ pt/1¼ cups white wine
15 ml/1 tbsp tomato purée (paste)
300 ml/½ pt/1¼ cups water
Salt and black pepper
8 olives, stoned (pitted)
8 slices of garlic sausage
50 g/2 oz/½ cup grated Parmesan cheese
50 g/2 oz/1 cup breadcrumbs

Method

1. Cook the beans in distilled water for 1 hour. Top up water to keep the beans covered and bubbling gently.

2. Remove any fat from the lamb and cut into 2.5 cm/1 in cubes. Dip in seasoned flour and shake off the surplus.

3. In a pan, heat the oil and brown the meat for 4 minutes. Remove and place in casserole dish (Dutch oven). In same pan, stir-fry the onion for 2 minutes, add the garlic, cook for 30 seconds and then add the wine and tomato purée. Boil for 3 minutes then add this liquid to the meat. Top up with water and add seasonings. Cover with a lid and braise in a preheated oven for 1½ hours at 180°C/350°F/gas mark 4.
(The beans could be cooked in the oven in a casserole dish at the same time, if you prefer).

4. Divide the stew between four individual earthenware bowls. Top up with beans, olives and garlic sausage. Sprinkle with grated cheese and breadcrumbs. Place bowls on a tray and bake in the oven to brown the top for 15 minutes at 200°C/400°F/gas mark 6.

Serves 4

Preparation time: 10 mins
Cooking time: 1½ hours

Lamb with Mixed Vegetables (Navarin d'Agneau aux Légumes)

Ingredients
30 ml/2 tbsp oil
450 g/1 lb stewing lamb, cubed
1 onion, chopped
225 g/8 oz fresh tomatoes, skinned, seeded and diced
3 garlic cloves, chopped
900 ml/1½ pts/3¾ cups water
1 sprig of thyme
10 ml/2 tsp salt, pepper and sugar
For the garnish:
225 g/8 oz mixed diced vegetables
(e.g. carrot, turnip, swede, peas)

Method

1. Heat the oil in a shallow pan and stir-fry the meat and onion for 8 minutes. Add the chopped tomatoes, garlic, water and thyme. Simmer for 1¼ hours until the meat is tender or cook in the oven at 160°C/325°F/gas mark 3.

2. Towards the end of the cooking time, boil separately diced vegetables of your choice. Strain and keep warm.

3. When the meat is cooked, strain the liquid into a saucepan and boil until it is reduced by half. Season with salt, pepper and sugar to taste and reheat the meat and cooked mixed vegetables in this reduced stock sauce.

4. Serve with boiled new potatoes and Creamed Aubergine.

Serves 4

Preparation time: 10 mins
Cooking time: 1¾ hours

Creamed Aubergines
(Aubergine à la Crème)

Ingredients
750 g/1½ lb aubergines (eggplant)
30 ml/2 tbsp butter
30 ml/2 tbsp plain (all-purpose) flour
250 ml/8 fl oz/1 cup milk
50 g/2 oz/½ cup strong cheese, grated
Salt and black pepper

Method
1. Grill the aubergines until the skin is blackened. Leave to cool slightly then peel off the skins.

2. Place the aubergines in a colander and press out the juices. Transfer the flesh to a blender and purée.

3. Melt the butter, stir in the flour and cook, stirring continuously, for 1 minute.

4. Remove from the heat and blend in the milk then return to the heat and bring to the boil, stirring continuously to avoid any lumps. Simmer gently for 5 minutes, stirring occasionally.

5. Stir in the aubergine purée and the cheese and season well with salt and pepper.

Serves 4

Preparation time: 3 mins
Cooking time: 20 mins

Chapter

8

Bacon and Pork Dishes

Bacon and Pork Dishes

All the Latin countries are known for their cured hams. The most famous ham comes from the Mediterranean countries. Spain has the excellent *jamon serrano* and Parma ham from Italy is perhaps the most exported meat in the world. In France both our Jambon de Bayonne and Ardennes are also renowned. In fact, throughout the region you will come across good quality ham.

Although for religious reasons, there are many people who cannot eat pork, there are as many, if not more, who are able to enjoy it, not least because it is one of the cheapest meats in many parts of the world. The Spaniards like it barbecued, the French enjoy their garlic sausages in stews and the Italians make it into one of the most sophisticated hors d'oeuvres — smoked ham with melon or fresh figs.

In this section there are popular but simple dishes using both cured ham and also fresh pork. Mediterranean cured hams are now readily available in supermarkets and delicatessens.

It is acknowledged that British pork is some of the best in Europe, so you will be able to appreciate these recipes even more when they are made with top quality meat.

Pork with Marsala
(Maiale al Marsala)

Ingredients
60 ml/4 tbsp olive oil
750 g /1½ lb pork fillet, sliced
Salt and pepper
200 ml/7 fl oz/scant 1 cup Marsala

Method

1. Heat the oil and fry (sauté) the pork until lightly browned on both sides.

2. Sprinkle with salt and pepper and stir in the Marsala.

3. Bring to the boil and simmer gently for about 15-20 minutes, stirring frequently, until the meat is cooked and the sauce has reduced. Add a little water during cooking if necessary.

Serves 4

Preparation time: 3 mins
Cooking time: 30 mins

Pork Cutlets with Peppers
(Côte de Porc aux Poivrons)

Ingredients
4 pork cutlets, boned and fat trimmed
Salt and black pepper
Plain (all-purpose) flour
45 ml/3 tbsp oil for shallow frying
1 onion, cut in fine strips
1 red, 1 green and 1 yellow (bell) pepper,
split, seeded and cut in fine strips
For the sauce:
15 ml/1 tbsp tomato purée (paste)
10 ml/2 tsp wine vinegar
5 ml/1 tsp sugar
300 ml/½ pt/1¼ cups water
10 ml/2 tsp cornflour (cornstarch)
1 pickled gherkin, cut in fine strips

Method
1. Rub the pork cutlets in seasoned flour. Shake off any surplus. Heat 30 ml/2 tbsp of the oil in a pan and brown pork cutlets for 1 minute on each side. Transfer the cutlets onto an earthenware dish.

2. Add the remaining oil and stir-fry the onion and peppers for 2 minutes. Remove from the pan and put on top of the pork cutlets.

3. Mix the sauce ingredients in a pan and boil for 2 minutes. Pour the sauce over the cutlets and peppers. Cover with a lid and braise for 30 minutes in preheated oven at 180°C/350°F/gas mark 4.

4. Serve with pickled gherkin strips on top of each cutlet.

Serves 4

Preparation time: 10 mins
Cooking time: 12 mins

Cured Ham and Leek Turnovers (Crôustade de Jambon de Bayonne aux Poireaux)

Ingredients
4 leeks, white part only
Salt
4 thin slices of cured ham, weighing 150 g/5 oz
150 g/5 oz sausagemeat
1 egg, beaten
15 ml/1 tbsp chopped parsley
450 g/1 lb puff pastry (paste)
1 egg yolk
45 ml/3 tbsp water
15 ml/1 tbsp sesame seeds

Method
1. Wash the leeks and split them. Boil for 5 minutes in salted water and drain. Squeeze off surplus water.

2. Wrap each leek in a slice of ham.

3. In a bowl blend the sausagemeat with the beaten egg and parsley.

4. Roll the puff pastry on a floured board to a thickness of 5 mm/¼ in and cut 4 rounds of 18 cm/7 in diameter. Brush the edges with water.

5. Divide the sausagemeat mixture into four, shape into a flat pancake and place each one in the centre of a pastry round. Place a roll of ham and leek on the sausagemeat. Fold the round over to make a semi-circle. Crimp the edges to seal the pastry.

6. Place the turnovers onto a greased baking sheet. Brush each one with egg yolk mixed with water and sprinkle sesame seeds on top. Rest at room temperature for 45 minutes, then bake in a preheated oven at 200°C/400°F/gas mark 6 for 15-20 minutes.

7. Serve hot or cold.

Serves 4

Preparation time: 10 mins
Cooking time: 15 mins

Pork Dumplings Sicilian-style (Polpette Siciliana)

Ingredients
450 g/1 lb lean pork, minced (ground)
60 ml/4 tbsp breadcrumbs
60 ml/4 tbsp chopped parsley
1 onion, chopped
2 garlic cloves, chopped
1 egg, beaten
Salt and pepper
60 ml/4 tbsp plain (all-purpose) flour
300 ml/½ pt/1¼ cups tomato juice
300 ml/½ pt/1¼ cups stock
1 red chilli (chili), seeded and chopped
30 ml/2 tbsp cornflour (cornstarch)
60 ml/4 tbsp water
Salt and pepper
225 g/8 oz/2 cups sweetcorn
60 ml/4 tbsp butter

Method
1. In a bowl, combine the pork, breadcrumbs, parsley, onion, garlic, egg and seasoning. Blend well and divide into 24 balls. Roll the balls in flour.

2. Bring the tomato juice, stock and chilli to the boil and half fill a shallow metal dish with this liquid. Simmer the dumplings for 15-20 minutes. Remove and keep hot in a dish.

3. Reboil the tomato stock and thicken it with a mixture of cornflour and water. Boil for 4 minutes. Season to taste.

4. Boil the sweetcorn for 5 minutes and drain. Flavour with a little butter and seasoning.

5. Serve the dumplings coated with the sauce and sweetcorn.

Serves 4

Preparation time: 8 mins
Cooking time: 15 minutes

Bacon Rice Pilaf Spanish-style (Arroz di Jamon)

Ingredients
8 rindless back bacon rashers (slices), diced
60 ml/4 tbsp olive oil
1 onion, chopped
2 garlic cloves, chopped
150 g/5 oz/scant ⅔ cup long-grain rice
600 ml/1 pt/2½ cups water
50 g/2 oz/½ cup fresh marrowfat peas
Salt and black pepper

Method
1. Heat the oil in a pan and stir-fry the bacon for 1 minute. Add the onion and garlic and cook for a further minute. Add the rice and stir to allow the rice to get well impregnated in bacon fat and oil.

2. Add water and marrowfat peas. Season and bring to the boil for 2 minutes. Transfer the contents to a shallow dish. Cover with greased foil or a lid and bake in a preheated oven for 20 minutes at 200°C/400°F/gas mark 6.

Serves 4

Preparation time: 5 mins
Cooking time: 20 mins

Barbecue Spare Ribs
(Poitrine de Porc a l'Aigré-Doux)

Ingredients
1 kg/2¼ lb pork spare ribs
For the barbecue marinade:
300 ml/½ pt/1¼ cups dry white wine
½ green chilli (chili), seeded and chopped
10 ml/2 tsp meat or yeast extract
30 ml/2 tbsp vinegar
30 ml/2 tbsp sugar
5 ml/1 tsp tomato purée (paste)
45 ml/3 tbsp olive oil
2 garlic cloves, chopped
30 ml/2 tbsp honey
2.5 ml/½ tsp mixed (apple pie) spice
2.5 ml/½ tsp ground anis seeds
2.5 ml/½ tsp ground ginger

Method
1. Put the spare ribs in cold water. Bring to the boil and simmer for 20 minutes. This helps to remove excess fat and tenderise the meat.

2. In a bowl, combine all the barbecue marinade ingredients. Stir well. Soak the cooked spare ribs in this sauce for 1 hour, turning from time to time. Transfer ribs and sauce onto a baking dish and bake in a moderate oven for 45 minutes at 180°C/350°F/gas mark 4. Turn the ribs from time to time until well glazed.

Serves 4

Preparation time: 10 mins
Cooking time: 1 hour

Roast Spiced Bacon Fillet
(Filet de Porc à la Mentonnaise)

Ingredients
400 g/14 oz lean back bacon in one piece
For the marinade sauce:
15 ml/1 tbsp meat or yeast extract
120 ml/4 fl oz/½ cup red vermouth
15 ml/1 tbsp honey
15 ml/1 tbsp sugar
15 ml/1 tbsp wine vinegar
1 small pickled beetroot
Juice and grated rind of 1 lemon
1 garlic clove, chopped
2.5 ml/½ tsp cinnamon
1 shallot, chopped
2.5 ml/½ tsp cornflour (cornstarch)
Salt and black pepper

Method
1. Trim the bacon of all skin.

2. Combine all the remaining ingredients and liquidise. Marinate the bacon for 1 hour in this sauce, or cover and refrigerate overnight.

3. Drain the bacon, keeping the marinade for later use.

4. Place the bacon on a trivet of bone or a rack over a baking sheet and roast in a moderate oven at 180°C/350°F/gas mark 4 for 30 minutes, basting it every 10 minutes with the marinade. Remove from the oven. Boil marinade for 3 minutes and serve it as a gravy. Cut the bacon slantwise like a salami. Serve with a mixed salad.

Serves 2

Preparation time: 8 mins
Cooking time: 30 mins

Loin Steak in Orange Sauce
(Médaillon de Porc à l'Orange)

Ingredients
2 loin steaks, 2.5 cm/1 in thick
Seasoned flour
45 ml/3 tbsp oil
1 shallot, chopped
1 carrot, chopped
1 celery stick (rib), chopped
5 ml/1 tsp tomato purée (paste)
5 ml/1 tsp dried mint
150 ml/5 fl oz/⅔ cup water
Juice and rind of 1 sweet orange
150 ml/5 fl oz/⅔ cup white port wine
5 ml/1 tsp vinegar
2 lumps of sugar
15 ml/1 tbsp cornflour (cornstarch)
60 ml/4 tbsp cold water
For the garnish:
8 orange segments

Method
1. Remove the fat from loin steaks. Rub in seasoned flour and shake off any surplus.

2. Heat 30 ml/2 tbsp of the oil in a pan and brown the loin on both sides. Reduce the heat and cover with a lid. Cook gently for 10 minutes.

3. In a pan, heat remaining oil and stir-fry the shallot, carrot and celery for 2 minutes. Add the tomato purée, mint, water, orange juice and port wine and boil for 4 minutes.

4. Thinly pare the orange and scald the rind in boiling water for 1 minute. Drain.

5. In a small frying pan (skillet) place the sugar and the vinegar. Heat until it turns a copper colour, like caramel, and immediately pour in a little of the sauce to prevent it from burning. (This last operation is important so have the sauce ready before the sugar is caramelised.) Return this liquid to the remaining sauce. Strain it. Reboil.

6. Mix the cornflour with the cold water and add this to the boiling sauce. Season to taste and add the strips of blanched orange rind.

7. Place the loin steaks in a shallow dish. Cover with orange sauce and garnish them with orange segments.

Serves 2

Preparation time: 8 mins
Cooking time: 12 mins

Chapter

9

Poultry Dishes

Poultry Dishes

There is a southern saying that if it flies, it's edible. In all the farming communities you will find geese and ducks preserved in their own fat. Hence the reason such birds are much preferred to chicken or turkey. Unless they have been specially fattened all the white-fleshed poultry tend to look scraggy when you see them on open markets, many still sold with feathers on.

But in countries where the Canard à l'Orange and Poule au Pot with truffles have been famous for centuries, many old dishes like Coq au Vin, Spanish duck Paella and stuffed goose with chestnut stuffing have firm followers. However, many cafés serve chicken and chips or with salads *al fresco* and the Algerian chicken couscous is an everyday dish in Marseilles.

On the whole free-range poultry has a better taste and it is thought that if the bird is lean and free of fat, the flavour is improved, but in chicken, as in duck and geese, it is the fat that produces the characteristic poultry taste, and this is heightened when the birds are barbecued or roasted on the spit, one of the most popular ways of cooking poultry in southern regions.

Chicken with Rosemary
(Pollo al Rosmarino)

This is a traditionally southern Italian dish.

Ingredients
50 g/2 oz/¼ cup butter
15 ml/1 tbsp olive oil
3 garlic cloves
3 sprigs fresh rosemary
4 chicken portions
Salt and black pepper
150-200 ml/5-7 fl oz/⅔-scant 1 cup dry white wine

Method
1. Melt the butter with the oil and fry (sauté) the garlic and 2 sprigs of rosemary for 2 minutes. Discard the garlic and rosemary. Add the chicken and fry until browned on all sides.

2. Season with salt and pepper and stir in most of the wine. Bring to a simmer, cover and simmer gently for about 40 minutes until the chicken is tender, stirring occasionally and adding the rest of the wine if the dish appears to be drying out too much.

3. Serve garnished with the reserved rosemary sprig.

Serves 4

Preparation time: 5 mins
Cooking time: 50 mins

Chicken with Raisins and Pine Nuts (Pollo con Pasas y Pinones)

Ingredients
45 ml/3 tbsp raisins
150 ml/¼ pt/⅔ cup dry sherry
30 ml/2 tbsp olive oil
15 ml/1 tbsp butter
4 chicken portions
Salt and black pepper
30 ml/2 tbsp pine nuts

Method
1. Soak the raisins in the sherry.

2. Heat most of the oil with the butter and fry (sauté) the chicken until lightly browned on all sides.

3. Season with salt and pepper then stir in the sherry and raisins. Cover and simmer gently for about 30 minutes until the chicken is cooked through and tender, stirring occasionally and adding a little water during cooking if necessary.

4. Fry the pine nuts in the remaining oil in a separate pan until golden. Drain on kitchen paper then stir into the chicken and serve with rice.

Serves 4

Preparation time: 5 mins
Cooking time: 40 mins

Chicken Sautéd with Peppers, Tomatoes and Mushrooms (Poulet Basquaise)

Ingredients
1.5 kg/3 lb roasting chicken
Seasoned flour
90 ml/6 tbsp cooking oil
1 large onion, cut in strips
1 red (bell) pepper, seeded and cut in strips
1 garlic clove
4 large mushrooms, cut in slices
300 ml/½ pt/1¼ cups dry white wine
150 ml/5 fl oz/⅔ cup water
5 ml/1 tsp yeast extract
Salt and black pepper
Sugar
30 ml/2 tbsp cornflour (cornstarch)
60 ml/4 tbsp water
4 tomatoes, skinned, seeded and chopped
30 ml/2 tbsp chopped tarragon

Method

1. Cut the chicken into eight pieces. Divide the legs in two and the breast in four portions, or buy chicken joints. Rub all the pieces in seasoned flour in a large mixing bowl. Shake off any surplus.

2. Heat 60 ml/4 tbsp of the oil in a large frying pan (skillet) or wok and brown the chicken pieces for 4 minutes, turning frequently. Transfer the chicken pieces to a shallow dish.

3. In the same pan, add 30 ml/2 tbsp of the oil and stir-fry the onion and pepper for 2 minutes. Add the garlic and mushrooms, stir for 30 seconds then add wine, water and yeast extract. Season to taste with salt, pepper and a little sugar to taste. Bring to the boil.

4. Mix together the cornflour and water and add to the boiling sauce. Boil for a further 2 minutes and add to the chicken with the chopped tomatoes and tarragon. Cover with a lid and braise for 40 minutes in a preheated oven at 180°C/350°F/gas mark 4.

Serves 4

Preparation time: 10 mins
Cooking time: 40 mins

Chicken Casserole with Chickpeas and Chilli (Cocido Barcelona)

Ingredients

100 g/4 oz/⅔ cup chickpeas (garbanzos)
1 oven-ready chicken, cut into eight portions
1 litre/1¾ pts/4¼ cups water
1 carrot, cut into chunks
1 onion, chopped
1 fennel bulb, sliced
15 ml/1 tbsp tomato purée (paste)
1 chilli (chili), sliced
2 garlic cloves
4 ml/¾ tsp ground cumin
Salt and black pepper
100 g/4 oz/½ cup long-grain rice
45 ml/3 tbsp chopped parsley or chervil

Method

1. Soak the chickpeas overnight and boil for 1½ hours. Alternatively, use canned chickpeas.

2. Place the chicken in a large pan covered with cold water. Bring to the boil and remove scum as it rises. After 10 minutes or when the broth is clear, add the raw vegetables and simmer gently for 20 minutes.

3. Add chickpeas, tomato purée, chilli, garlic and ground cumin. Simmer for a further ten minutes. Place vegetables and chicken in a shallow dish.

4. Boil the rice in the chicken stock for 17 minutes. Drain, season and serve with chicken and vegetables together with a little of the stock. Sprinkle fresh parsley on top.

Oven-ready roasting chickens do not take long to stew in clear liquid, but old birds would take about 1½ hours.

Serves 4

Preparation time: 10 mins
Cooking time: 30 mins

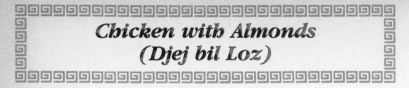

Chicken with Almonds
(Djej bil Loz)

This is a North African dish.

Ingredients
4 chicken pieces
300 ml/½ pt/1¼ cups water
100 g/4 oz/1 cup almonds
2 onions, thinly sliced
75 ml/5 tbsp olive oil
2.5 ml/½ tsp cinnamon
2.5 ml/½ tsp ground ginger
Pinch of saffron
1 large bunch of fresh parsley, finely chopped
sprigs of parsley to garnish

Method
1. Place all the ingredients except the parsley in a large pan. Bring to the boil, cover and simmer gently for at least 1 hour until the chicken is very tender, stirring occasionally and adding a little more water during cooking if necessary.

2. Add the chopped parsley and simmer for a further few minutes.

3. Serve hot, garnished with the fresh parsley.

Serves 4

Preparation time: 5 mins
Cooking time: 1¼ hours

Sweet Chicken with Tomatoes (Djej Matisha Mesla)

Ingredients
4 chicken portions
45 ml/3 tbsp olive oil
Salt and pepper
1 onion, finely chopped
2 garlic cloves, chopped
1.1 kg/2½ lb tomatoes, skinned and roughly chopped
10 ml/2 tsp ground ginger
45 ml/3 tbsp clear honey
15 ml/1 tbsp sesame seeds

Method
1. Place the chicken, oil, salt, pepper, onion, garlic, tomatoes and ginger in a large pan. Simmer over a low heat, stirring frequently, for about 1 hour until the chicken is very tender.

2. Remove the chicken from the pan and keep it warm.

3. Increase the heat under the sauce and stir carefully until the sauce thickens and darkens, taking care that it does not burn.

4. Stir in the honey. Return the chicken to the sauce to heat through and make sure the chicken is coated with the sauce.

5. Meanwhile, toast the sesame seeds in a dry frying pan (skillet) until lightly browned.

6. Transfer the chicken to a warmed serving dish and serve garnished with the sesame seeds.

Serves 4

Preparation time: 5 mins
Cooking time: 1¼ hours

Lemon Chicken Breasts
(Polo di Lemone Mentonese)

Ingredients
2 large breasts of chicken
60 ml/4 tbsp seasoned flour
2 eggs, beaten
45 ml/3 tbsp water
50 g/2 oz/½ cup plain (all-purpose) flour
Salt and pepper
Oil for frying
150 ml/5 fl oz/⅔ cup medium dry sherry
Juice and grated rind of 1 lemon
1 chicken stock cube
1 shallot, chopped
15 ml/1 tbsp chopped lemon grass
Salt and pepper
1 small piece green ginger or 4 ml/¾ tsp ground
ginger
30 ml/2 tbsp honey
30 ml/2 tbsp sugar
5 ml/1 tsp vinegar
2 egg yolks
5 ml/1 tsp cornflour (cornstarch)
120 ml/4 fl oz/½ cup single (light) cream
4 spring onions (scallions), cut slantwise

Method
1. Remove the skin and bone from the breasts of chicken.
Flatten the flesh and cut each breast into four pieces. Dip in
seasoned flour.

2. Prepare an egg batter with the eggs, flour and water. Season.

3. Dip the chicken pieces in batter, drain well and fry (sauté)
in hot oil until lightly golden and cooked through.

4. Drain on kitchen paper, place in a shallow dish and keep warm while preparing a lemon sauce.

5. Boil the sherry, lemon juice, rind, shallot and lemon grass with the ginger, honey, sugar and vinegar for 3 minutes.

6. Mix the egg yolks, cornflour and cream in a bowl and add 1 cup of the sherry sauce while whisking.

7. Pour this egg mixture into the remaining sherry liquid and bring it to the boil for 2 minutes. Season to taste. Strain and pour over the chicken pieces.

8. Sprinkle with spring onions.

Serves 2

Preparation time: 10 mins
Cooking time: 10 mins

Breast of Chicken with Garlic Cheese (Suprême de Volaille à la Corsicane)

Ingredients
2 breasts of chicken
75 g/3 oz/⅓ cup cream cheese
25 g/1 oz/1¼ cup breadcrumbs
1 garlic clove, chopped
15 ml/1 tbsp chopped parsley
Salt and 1.5 ml/¼ tsp coarsely milled black pepper
Seasoned flour
1 egg, beaten
75 g/3 oz/1½ cups breadcrumbs and cornmeal mixed
Oil for shallow-frying

Method
1. Remove the skin, bone and underfillet from the chicken. Wet the chicken and, using a mallet, gently flatten the breasts like an escalope. This can be done between two sheets of polythene but care must be taken so as not to tear the flesh.

2. Blend the cream cheese with the breadcrumbs, garlic and parsley and season to taste. Divide the mixture into two and roll into a sausage-shape. Put this in the centre of the chicken breast with the underfillet on top, and roll up the breasts, like a cigar. Dip in seasoned flour, beaten egg and breadcrumbs and cornmeal mix.

3. Heat the oil in a pan and shallow fry the chicken for 8 minutes until golden and cooked through. Drain well on kitchen paper and serve with a tossed green salad.

Serves 2

Preparation time: 10 mins
Cooking time: 15 mins

Chicken with Fennel
(Blanc de Poulet au Fenouil)

Ingredients
2 breasts of chicken, skinned and boned
750 ml/1¼ pts/3 cups water
1 chicken stock cube
4 ml/¾ tsp ground ginger
5 ml/1 tsp anis seeds or dill (dillweed)
1 fennel bulb, sliced
30 ml/2 tbsp white vinegar
Salt and pepper
10 ml/2 tsp sugar
1 celery stick (rib), cut in chunks
For the salad dressing:
45 ml/3 tbsp olive oil
Juice of 1 lemon
5 ml/1 tsp made Dijon mustard
15 ml/1 tbsp chopped parsley
75 ml/5 tbsp chicken liquor
50 g/2 oz/½ cup toasted sesame seeds

Method
1. Place the two chicken breasts side by side in a casserole dish (Dutch oven). Cover with water, add the stock cube, ginger, anis seeds, fennel, vinegar, salt and pepper and sugar. Bring to the boil and simmer for 20 minutes. Cool and cut in small pieces.

2. In half of the chicken stock, cook the celery for 2 minutes, remove while still crunchy and pat dry.

3. Whisk the salad dressing ingredients. Add 250 ml/8 fl oz/ 1 cup of strained chicken stock and pour over the chicken. Garnish with celery chunks and toasted sesame seeds.

Serves 2

Preparation time: 5 mins
Cooking time: 15 mins

Turkey and Chestnut Rolls (Roulade de Dinde Toulousaine)

Ingredients
750g/1½ lb breast of turkey, skinned and boned
Plain (all-purpose) flour
Salt and pepper
150 g/5 oz lean minced (ground) pork
75 g/3 oz/⅓ cup peeled and semi-boiled chestnuts, chopped
1 egg, beaten
15 ml/1 tbsp chopped parsley
50 g/2 oz/¼ cup mixture of butter and oil
100 g/4 oz/1 cup cranberries
1 apple, peeled and sliced
10 ml/2 tsp sugar
5 ml/1 tsp cinnamon
300 ml/½ pt/1¼ cups water

Method

1. Cut the breast laterally in four slices. Dust with flour and seasoning.

2. In a bowl, combine minced pork with chestnuts, egg and parsley. Season to taste. Spread this filling over each escalope. Roll and tie up with string.

3. Heat the oil and butter in a shallow pan and brown the four rolls for 5 minutes. Transfer to a shallow dish. Cover with water and bake in the oven for 20 minutes at 200°C/400°F/gas mark 6. Remove the rolls and discard the strings.

4. Strain the turkey liquor into a pan with the cranberries and apple. Cook for 8 minutes. Season with sugar, cinnamon and a pinch of salt. Liquidise the mixture to a very thin purée, adding as much of the water as you need.

Serves 4

Preparation time: 10 mins
Cooking time: 15 mins

Chicken and Prawn Neapolitan-style (Pollo con Scamponi Napoli)

Ingredients
3 large boneless chicken breasts without skin, cut into 18 pieces
15 ml/1 tbsp and 5 ml/1 tsp cornflour (cornstarch)
1 red (bell) pepper, deseeded and cut in small squares
6 shallots, chopped
45 ml/3 tbsp vegetable oil
120 ml/4 fl oz/½ cup chicken stock or water
5 ml/1 tsp salt and 1.5 ml/¼ tsp white ground pepper
15 ml/1 tbsp tomato purée (paste)
5 ml/1 tsp sugar
12 small peeled prawns (shrimp)
8 spring onions (scallions), cut 4 cm/1½ in long
45 ml/3 tbsp water
Juice of 1 lemon

Method
1. Rub the chicken with 15 ml/1 tbsp of cornflour.

2. In a large frying pan, heat the oil and fry chicken for about 6 minutes until golden brown. Add the red pepper and shallots and stir-fry for 1 minute.

3. Pour in the chicken stock (or water), tomato purée, sugar, salt and pepper, peeled prawns and spring onions. Cover pan with a lid and simmer for 5 minutes.

4. Thicken the sauce with 5 ml/1 tsp cornflour diluted with the water. Stir until boiling. Taste for seasoning and add the lemon juice. Serve on a bed of plain boiled long-grain rice.

Serves 4

Preparation time: 10 mins
Cooking time: 12 mins

Duck with Pears
(Pato con Peras)

Using fruit with duck gives a good contrast to the rich flavour of the meat. The recipe can also be made with goose. The garlic and almond paste is a traditional Spanish way of thickening and flavouring sauces.

Ingredients
1 large oven-ready duck, cut into 6 pieces
60 ml/4 tbsp olive oil
6 firm pears, peeled and halved
1 cinnamon stick
3 onions, sliced
1 carrot, sliced
3 tomatoes, skinned, seeded and chopped
5 ml/1 tsp chopped fresh thyme
Salt and black pepper
100 ml/3½ fl oz/6½ tbsp brandy
300 ml/½ pt/1¼ cups chicken stock
3 garlic cloves, chopped
50 g/2 oz/½ cup flaked almonds

Method
1. Fry (sauté) the duck in 30 ml/2 tbsp of the oil until browned on all sides . Discard the excess fat.

2. Meanwhile, place the pears in a pan and just cover with water. Add the cinnamon and simmer gently for about 15 minutes until only just tender. Drain and reserve 300 ml/½ pt/ 1¼ cups of the cooking water. Discard the cinnamon and keep the pears warm.

3. Heat the remaining oil and fry the onions, carrot and tomatoes until soft. Add the thyme and brandy and season with salt and pepper. Stir in the stock and reserved cooking liquid and simmer for 25 minutes.

4. Purée the sauce then return it to the pan and add the duck. Simmer gently for about 50 minutes until the duck is tender and the sauce has thickened slightly.

5. Place the garlic and almonds in a blender and process to a thick paste. Stir into the sauce and simmer for a further 15 minutes, stirring frequently.

6. Transfer to a warmed serving platter and serve garnished with the warm pears.

Serves 4

Preparation time: 10 mins
Cooking time: 1½ hours

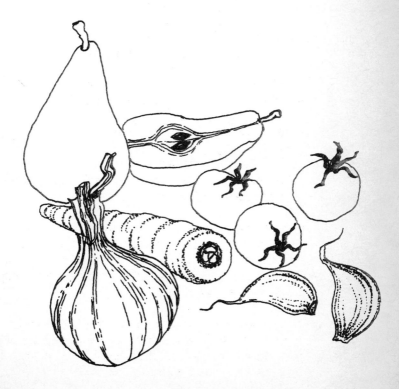

Duck with Broccoli and Almonds (Canard au Broccoli)

Ingredients
450 g/1 lb breast of duck, cubed and skin removed
50 g/2 oz/½ cup plain (all-purpose) flour
Salt and pepper
2.5 ml/½ tsp cinnamon
100 ml/3½ fl oz/6½ tbsp oil
50 g/2 oz/½ cup onion, sliced
225 g/8 oz broccoli florets, chopped
100 g/4 oz red (bell) pepper, seeded and cut in strips
100 g/4 oz/1 cup mushrooms, sliced
150 ml/5 fl oz/⅔ cup dry white wine
5 ml/1 tsp cornflour (cornstarch)
15 ml/1 tbsp water
45 ml/3 tbsp toasted almonds

Method
1. Wash the duck, pat dry and cut in 1 cm/½" cubes. Toss in seasoned flour mixed with cinnamon.

2. Heat half the oil in a shallow pan and stir-fry for 6 minutes. Remove from the pan and keep warm. Drain off the pan.

3. Add the remainder of the oil and stir-fry the onion for 1 minute, then add the other vegetables and cook for 2 minutes. Stir the wine into the vegetables and boil for 3 minutes.

4. Mix the cornflour with water and add to the pan. Boil for 1 minute. Season to taste. Sprinkle with toasted almonds.

Serves 2

Preparation time: 10 mins
Cooking time: 15 mins

Duck Strips in Lime Sauce
(Julienne de Canard)

Ingredients
450 g/1 lb breast of duck, skinned
100 g/4 oz/1 cup flour
Salt and pepper
1 egg, beaten
2 egg yolks
150 ml/5 fl oz/⅔ cup milk
60 ml/4 tbsp oil
50 g/2 oz/½ cup onion, chopped
150 ml/5 fl oz/⅔ cup chicken stock
5 ml/1 tsp honey
45 ml/3 tbsp lime juice and grated rind
5 ml/1 tsp cornflour (cornstarch) and
20 ml/4 tsp water mixed

Method
1. Cut the breast of duck into thin strips and toss in a little of the flour seasoned with salt and pepper.

2. Make a batter by combining the whole egg, remaining flour and milk in a bowl. Mix well and add seasoning.

3. Heat half the oil in a shallow pan, dip the duck pieces in the batter and fry for about 4 minutes until they are crisp. Drain on kitchen paper.

4. To make the sauce, heat the remainder of the oil in a pan and stir-fry the onion for 1 minute. Drain off the oil and add chicken stock. Boil for 3 minutes, then add honey, lime juice and rind.

5. In a cup blend the 2 egg yolks with the cornflour and water. Add to the stock and continue boiling for 4 minutes. Season to taste. Strain the sauce.

Serves 2

Preparation time: 10 mins
Cooking time: 10 mins

Chicken Burger
(Cromeski de Poulet)

Ingredients
2 chicken breasts
60 ml/4 tbsp double (heavy) cream
60 ml/4 tbsp breadcrumbs
1 egg, beaten
Salt and white pepper
Plain (all-purpose) flour
60 ml/4 tbsp butter and oil mixed
4 spring onions (scallions), sliced slantwise
100 g/4 oz/1 cup button mushrooms, sliced
15 ml/1 tbsp chopped mixed herbs: basil, parsley, taragon
Salt and pepper

Method
1. Remove the bone and skin and mince (grind) the chicken meat. Combine the minced chicken with cream, breadcrumbs, egg and seasoning. Mix well.

2. Divide the mixture into four balls. Roll in flour and shape into burgers.

3. Heat half the butter and oil in a frying pan (skillet) and fry the burgers for 5 minutes on each side.

4. Remove the burgers from the pan. Using the remainder of the butter and oil, stir-fry the onions and mushrooms for 2 minutes. Season, add the herbs. Divide the mixture between four plates, placing a burger on top of each one.

Serves 4

Preparation time: 8 mins
Cooking time: 10 mins

Chapter

10

Vegetable Dishes

Vegetable Dishes

Plain boiled potatoes and cabbage would never do for the people of southern Europe where an exciting range of vegetables is grown and turned into dishes of infinite variety. All those who have visited this region and have tried baby globe artichokes in lemon dressing or sautéd green beans with smoked Parma ham know what it is like to taste the sun in their mouths. The numerous ways of cooking courgettes and aubergines can only be sampled in the kitchens of the countryside where the strong scent of basil mixes with a vast range of other herbs and spices to make a simple vegetable dish full of aromatic fragrance.

Such is the choice available to the cooks of the Mediterranean region that their vegetable dishes become a riot of colour with the brilliant red tomatoes, purple aubergines and peppers of red, yellow, purple and green. A vegetable course, thus, becomes a meal rather than just an accompaniment to a meat dish.

Fried Aubergine with Sesame Seeds
(Aubergines Frites aux Graines de Sésame)

Ingredients

2 aubergines (eggplants), cut in 1 cm/½ in slices slantwise
Salt and black pepper
Olive oil
15 ml/1 tbsp sesame paste
15 ml/1 tbsp wine vinegar
15 ml/1 tbsp honey
2 garlic cloves, chopped
60 ml/4 tbsp flour
2 eggs, beaten
60 ml/4 tbsp sesame seeds

Method

1. Slice the aubergine slantwise without peeling as the flavour is in the skin. Sprinkle salt over and leave for 30 minutes to remove the bitter juice. Wash the slices, drain and pat dry.

2. First prepare a purée garnish by heating 15 ml/1 tbsp oil in a frying pan (skillet) and stir-frying half the aubergine slices until soft. Add 45 ml/3 tbsp of olive oil and season to taste. Purée the mixture. Season with salt and pepper and add the sesame paste, wine vinegar and honey. Put in a small bowl.

3. To make the aubergine fritters, chop the garlic finely with 2.5 ml/½ tsp salt, add the flour and mix well. Dip the slices of aubergine in this mixture, then into beaten eggs and rub in sesame seeds.

4. Heat the oil and shallow fry for 30 seconds on each side. Drain well. Serve with aubergine purée as a dip.

Serves 2

Preparation time: 5 mins
Cooking time: 4 mins

Asparagus and Smoked Ham (Asparagi Italiana con Prosciutto)

Ingredients
1 bunch of 8 thin asparagus
2 thin slices of smoked Parma ham
2 thin slices of Mozarella cheese
Salt and black pepper

Method

1. Scrape the stalks of asparagus very lightly. Wash and tie in a bundle with a string. Cook in salted water in a deep metal roasting tin (pan) for 8 minutes. Remove, drain and pat dry. Discard the string.

2. Wrap four asparagus with a long slice of smoked ham to form a parcel. Place in a flameproof dish. Cover with a slice of Mozarella. Sprinkle with salt and black pepper.

3. Grill (broil) until the cheese has melted.

Serves 2

Preparation time: 5 mins
Cooking time: 8 mins

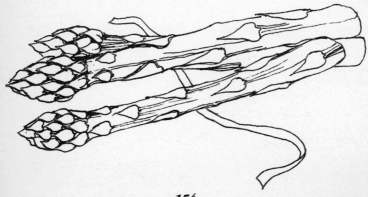

Tossed French Green Beans with Ham (Haricots Verts Antiboise)

Ingredients
**450 g/1 lb French beans, topped and tailed
45 ml/3 tbsp olive oil
1 celery stick (rib), cut in thin strips
Salt and black pepper
100 g/4 oz/½ cup lean cured ham, cut in thin strips
50 g/2 oz/½ cup flaked toasted almonds**

Method
1. Wash the beans and cook in salted water for 8 minutes. Drain and refresh in iced water to restore the green colour. Drain again.

2. In a large pan or wok, heat the oil and stir-fry the celery for 1 minute. Add the beans and toss for 3 minutes until hot. Season to taste. Finally add the ham strips and cook for 30 seconds.

3. Sprinkle over toasted flaked almonds.

<u>Serves 2</u>

Preparation time: 5 mins
Cooking time: 10 mins

Green Cabbage Sicilian-style (Cavolo Verdi Amarati)

Ingredients
½ green cabbage, core removed and finely shredded
45 ml/3 tbsp olive oil
45 ml/3 tbsp wine vinegar
15 ml/1 tbsp sweet vermouth
45 ml/3 tbsp small pickled capers
2 small onions, chopped
15 ml/1 tbsp caraway seeds
8 black olives, stoned (pitted)
Salt and pepper
2.5 ml/½ tsp sugar

Method
1. Wash the shredded cabbage and drain well. Cook in salted boiling water for 8 minutes.

2. Combine the remaining ingredients in a bowl.

3. Drain the cabbage well and toss in the dressing. Serve hot.

<u>Serves 2</u>

Preparation time: 5 mins
Cooking time: 8 mins

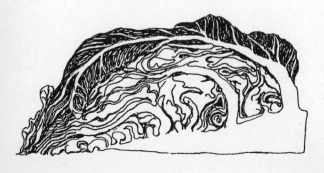

Sautéd Carrots with Honey
(Carotte en Gargotte)

Ingredients
2 large carrots, cut thinly slantwise
2 green celery sticks (ribs), cut slantwise 1 cm/½ in thick
45 ml/3 tbsp olive oil
1 small onion, cut in thin slices
15 ml/1 tbsp honey or ginger syrup
Salt and black pepper
1.5 ml/¼ tsp mixed (apple pie) spice
30 ml/2 tbsp roughly chopped parsley or chervil

Method
1. Scald the carrot and celery slices for 2 minutes in boiling salted water. Drain well.

2. Heat the oil in a large frying pan (skillet) and stir-fry the onion, celery and carrots for 2 minutes. Stir in the honey and season to taste with salt, black pepper and mixed spice. Sprinkle over chopped parsley and serve.

Serves 2

Preparation time: 5 mins
Cooking time: 5 mins

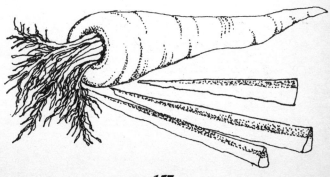

157

Cauliflower with Garlic Crumbs (Chou-Fleur Maltaise)

Ingredients
1 small cauliflower divided into small florets
1 hard-boiled (hard-cooked) egg, sieved or finely chopped
45 ml/3 tbsp chopped parsley and coriander leaves
15 ml/1 tbsp celery seeds
Salt and pepper
120 ml/4 fl oz/½ cup olive oil
75 g/3 oz/1½ cups white breadcrumbs
1.5 ml/¼ tsp curry powder
Juice of 1 lemon

Method
1. Soak the cauliflower in cold water for 20 minutes. Drain. Cook in boiling salted water for 10 minutes. Drain well and place in a shallow dish. Keep warm while preparing the dressing mixture.

2. Combine the egg, parsley, coriander, celery seeds, salt and black pepper.

3. Heat the oil in a frying pan (skillet) and fry the crumbs and curry powder for 30 seconds until golden. Cover the cauliflower sprigs with the crumbs, sprinkle the egg mixture over and serve with a squeeze of lemon juice.

Serves 4

Preparation time: 5 mins
Cooking time: 12 mins

Fennel with Bacon, Cheese and Tomato (Finocchi Gratinati)

Ingredients
1 fennel bulb, cut in half lengthwise
2 rashers (slices) of rindless back bacon, cut in strips
2 tomatoes, skinned, seeded and roughly chopped
50 g/2 oz/½ cup grated Gruyère cheese
(any other hard cheese is suitable)
Salt and black pepper

Method
1. Boil the fennel in salted water for 15 minutes. Drain, saving half a cup of the liquid.

2. Grill (broil) the bacon for 2 minutes. Wrap each half of fennel with a bacon rasher and place in individual shallow dishes. Cover completely with chopped tomatoes and season to taste.

3. Sprinkle with grated cheese and bake with 120 ml/4 fl oz/½ cup of fennel stock for 15 minutes in a preheated oven at 200°C/400°F/gas mark 6.

Serves 2

Preparation time: 5 mins
Cooking time: 30 mins

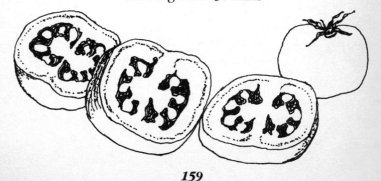

Sweet and Sour Courgette and Tomato (Caponata di Zucchini Agro Dolce)

Ingredients
1 green (bell) pepper, deseeded
75 ml/5 tbsp olive oil
1 onion, sliced
1 garlic clove, chopped
4 courgettes (zucchini), cut slantwise 1 cm/½ in thick
4 plum tomatoes, skinned, seeded and cut in halves
8 green olives, stoned (pitted)
45 ml/3 tbsp honey
45 ml/3 tbsp wine vinegar
120 ml/4 fl oz/½ cup water
Salt and pepper
7.5 ml/½ tbsp cornflour (cornstarch)
45 ml/3 tbsp water
Coriander (cilantro) leaves, roughly chopped

Method
1. Cut the green pepper in half. Remove seeds. Grill (broil) skin until it blisters then peel. Cut into very thin strips.

2. Heat the oil in a large pan and stir-fry the pepper for 1 minute. Add the onion, garlic and courgettes. Toss for 1 minute only then cover with tomatoes and green olives. Add the honey, vinegar, water and the seasoning. Bring to the boil.

3. Mix together the cornflour and water and add to the mixture. Boil for a further 4 minutes. Serve hot or cold with grilled chicken or fish. Sprinkle chopped herbs on serving.

Serves 2

Preparation time: 8 mins
Cooking time: 5 mins

Mushrooms with Garlic and Herbs (Gratin de Champignons en Aillade)

Ingredients
225 g/8 oz field mushrooms (bolito, ceps, etc)
225 g/8 oz new potatoes, peeled and sliced
90 ml/6 tbsp oil
1 onion, chopped
2 garlic cloves, chopped
45 ml/3 tbsp chopped parsley
8 spinach leaves, washed, drained and shredded
15 ml/1 tbsp chopped tarragon
Salt and black pepper
50 g/2 oz/1 cup breadcrumbs
50 g/2 oz/½ cup grated Parmesan cheese or any hard cheese

Method
1. Clean the mushrooms, wash and pat dry with a cloth. Slice the caps and stalks.

2. Boil the sliced new potatoes for 6 minutes. Drain.

3. Heat 60 ml/4 tbsp of oil in a pan and sauté the potatoes for 2 minutes. Add the mushrooms and toss for 1 minute. Transfer the mixture to two individual gratin dishes.

4. Heat remaining oil in the pan and stir-fry the onion and garlic for 1 minute then add the herbs and spinach.

5. Pour over the potato and mushroom mixture and season to taste. Sprinkle with grated cheese and breadcrumbs and brown under the grill (broiler) for 3 minutes.

Serves 2

Preparation time: 8 mins
Cooking time: 15 mins

Baked Potato Stuffed with Ricotta (Patates con Ricotta)

Ingredients
4 large potatoes, each 225 g/8 oz
175 g/6 oz/¾ cup Ricotta or cream cheese
1 egg, beaten
30 ml/2 tbsp breadcrumbs
50 g/2 oz/¼ cup butter
2 garlic cloves, chopped
30 ml/2 tbsp chopped chives
30 ml/2 tbsp chopped chervil
Juice and grated rind of ½ lemon
Salt and pepper
50 g/2 oz/½ cup flaked almonds
50 g/2 oz/½ cup grated Parmesan cheese

Method
1. Make a circular incision around the potato lengthwise. Wrap the potato in foil and bake in a preheated oven at 200°C/ 400°F/gas mark 6 for 1 hour or until cooked. Remove the foil and cut the potatoes in half. Scoop the pulp into a bowl, leaving a thick shell.

2. In a bowl, mash the potato pulp with the cream cheese, egg, breadcrumbs, butter, garlic, chives, chervil, lemon juice and the seasoning. Fill the potato shell. Sprinkle over flaked almonds and grated cheese. Rebake in the oven for 8 minutes.

Serves 4

Preparation time: 5 mins
Cooking time: 1 hour

Potato Tart with Onions and Pine Nuts (Torta Tarantina)

Ingredients
225 g/8 oz potatoes
1 small onion, finely chopped
2 eggs, beaten
30 ml/2 tbsp plain (all-purpose) flour
120 ml/4 fl oz/½ cup milk
60 ml/4 tbsp pine nuts, chopped
30 ml/2 tbsp chopped parsley
60 ml/4 tbsp oil
Salt and pepper

Method
1. Coarsely grate the potatoes, place in a cloth and squeeze the juice out.

2. In a bowl, combine the grated pulp with chopped onion, beaten egg, flour, milk, pine nuts and parsley.

3. Heat 15 ml/1 tbsp of oil in the pan. When smoking hot pour in one quarter of the mixture and cook for 4 minutes on each side over a moderate heat. Season with salt and black pepper.

4. Repeat with the remaining mixture to give four pancakes. While cooking press the mixture down with a fish slice to achieve a crisp finish.

Serves 2

Preparation time: 8 mins
Cooking time: 5 mins

163

Spinach with Garlic, Anchovy and Parmesan Cheese (Spinaci Lombardi)

Ingredients
450 g/1 lb young spinach leaves
60 ml/4 tbsp olive oil
2 garlic cloves, chopped
4 anchovy fillets, chopped
60 ml/4 tbsp fried bread croûtons
50 g/2 oz/½ cup grated Gruyère cheese
50 g/2 oz/½ cup grated Parmesan cheese
Salt and black pepper
2 hard-boiled (hard-cooked) eggs,
sieved or finely chopped

Method
1. Wash the spinach leaves and the stalks three times (the stalks should be cut into small pieces and used). Drain, and dry in a clean cloth. Squeeze out as much moisture as possible.

2. In a pan, heat the oil and toss the spinach for about 4 minutes until moisture has evaporated. Add the garlic, chopped anchovy, croûtons and grated Gruyère.
Season to taste.

3. Serve sprinkled with grated Parmesan cheese and egg.

Serves 2

Preparation time: 5 mins
Cooking time: 4 mins

Risotto Cooked in Wine (Risotto Milanese)

The difference between a rice pilaf and a risotto is that a pilaf is always cooked in the oven and is drier than the risotto which is cooked on top of the stove.

Ingredients
45 ml/3 tbsp olive oil
1 small onion, chopped
2 strands saffron
100 g/4 oz/½ cup long-grain rice
300 ml/½ pt/1¼ cups water
1 chicken stock cube
60 ml/4 tbsp sweet vermouth
50 g/2 oz/½ cup grated Parmesan cheese
50 g/2 oz/½ cup grated Gruyère cheese
Salt and black pepper

Method
1. Heat the oil in a thick-bottomed saucepan. Stir-fry the onion on a low heat for 2 minutes without browning. Add the saffron and rice and stir for 30 seconds, then add the water, stock cube, vermouth and seasoning and cook for 20 to 25 minutes, stirring from time to time.

2. When cooked, stir in the grated cheeses.
Serve with kebabs or with veal.

Serves 2

Preparation time: 5 mins
Cooking time: 20 mins

Chapter

11

Desserts and Sweets

Desserts and Sweets

The pastry cooks of Sicily are world famous and have perfected their art to such a high degree of excellence as to have influenced other members of the profession in all the Mediterranean countries. The Sicilians introduced their sorbets and ice creams to Paris in the 17th century and have never stopped improving their art.

But when the average family eats at home, the dessert is often cheese, figs, grapes or nuts and only on Sunday do they have a special gâteau, or torte or flan. The Italian waiters more than anybody else have made the Zabaione Marsala as famous as the French have with their chocolate eclairs.

You do not need more than a little wine to enjoy fresh strawberries or raspberries or peaches, far better than smothering them in cream. Figs in fortified sweet vermouth are a dream and pears in chocolate sauce, a classic and I doubt if we will ever get tired of fruit sorbets and ice cream.

As a trained chef and patissier I offer you in this section my selection of what I consider to be the most interesting 'entremets' as we call them in France: a rich apple and pear pumpkin tart, enriched pine nuts and seedless raisins and flavoured with Marsala; a walnut cake; a fried mixed fruit tartlet; a meringue trifle known as Zuppa Dolce; an open tart containing all the most colourful summer fruits and berries. This fantastico array of fruity desserts is enough to make any child stop eating chips! In all recipes the amount of sugar can always be cut without affecting the balance. Cream can be replaced by meringue, for dairy creams are probably more fattening than eating sugar by the bag full. In all cases, polyunsaturated vegetable margarine is as good as butter.

Meringue Ice Cake
(Gâteau Glacé Meringue)

Ingredients

25 g/1 oz/30 ml/2 tbsp glacé (candied) cherries,
orange peel and angelica
15 ml/1 tbsp orange liqueur
Butter, for greasing
1 small jam Swiss (jelly) roll, sliced
300 ml/½ pt/1¼ cups dairy ice cream
4 egg whites
175 g/6 oz/¾ cup granulated sugar
225 g/8 oz/2 cups fresh strawberries, sliced

Method

1. Cut the glacé fruits in small cubes. Soak them in the orange
liqueur for 15 minutes.

2. Butter a metal charlotte mould (mold) (600 ml/1 pt/2½ cup
capacity). Line the bottom and sides with greaseproof (waxed)
paper and grease it with butter. Line the mould with Swiss roll
slices, making sure the sponge sticks to the wall of the mould.

3. Soften some dairy ice cream quickly with a wooden spoon
and blend in the glacé fruits. Fill the mould. Cover with
greased foil and freeze overnight.

4. In a clean bowl, whisk the egg whites until they are stiff,
then add the sugar 1 spoonful at a time, whisking between
each addition. If you blend the sugar too quickly the meringue
will collapse.

5. Unmould the iced pudding and coat it with meringue, and
smooth with a palette knife. Sprinkle a little granulated sugar all
over. Bake for 8 minutes in a preheated oven at 200°C/400°F/
gas mark 6 until light brown to allow the meringue to set.

6. Decorate the pudding with sliced strawberries and serve.

Serves 6

Preparation time: 15 minutes
Cooking time: 8 mins

Blackcurrant Pudding
(Mousse au Cassis)

Ingredients
**225 g/8 oz/2 cups cooking (tart) apples, peeled,
cored and sliced
450 g/1 lb blackcurrants, half for sauce
and half for garnish
100 g/4 oz/½ cup caster (superfine) sugar
2 egg yolks
15 g/½ oz/1 tbsp gelatine (gelatin)
300 ml/½ pt/1¼ cups whipping cream**

Method
1. In a saucepan, cook the apples, half the currants and the sugar for 5 minutes until soft. Pass mixture through a sieve (strainer). Blend the egg yolks and gelatine with the sieved ingredients and reheat until it begins to bubble. Leave in saucepan for 2 minutes, then pour into a dish and cool on ice.

2. Blend the cream into the mousse and fill four moulds (molds) 200 ml/7 fl oz/scant 1 cup capacity. Chill. Just before serving decorate mousse with blackcurrants dusted with icing (confectioners') sugar. Serve with almond macaroons.

Serves 4

Preparation time: 10 mins plus chilling
Cooking time: 5 mins

Italian Bread Pudding
(Pane Dolci)

Ingredients
100 g/4 oz/½ cup soft unsalted butter
100 g/5 oz/⅔ cup caster (superfine) sugar
50 g/2 oz/4 slices brown bread, without crust
100 g/4 oz/⅔ cup sultanas (golden raisins),
soaked in 30 ml/2 tbsp of hot rum
300 ml/½ pt/1¼ cups single (light) cream
2 eggs, standard
2 drops each orange and lemon essence (extract)

Method
1. Butter the bottom of four 200 ml/7 fl oz capacity
ovenproof moulds (molds).

2. Put 25g/1 oz/2 tbsp of sultanas in each mould.

3. Cut four rounds of brown bread to fit the moulds and
spread with butter. Place one in each mould.

4. In a bowl beat the two eggs with 50 g/2 oz/¼ cup of caster
sugar, then blend in the cream. Add the orange and lemon
essences. Fill each mould with the cream mixture.

5. Bake in a deep pan half filled with hot water at
180°C/350°F/gas mark 4 for 20 minutes. Sprinkle over the
remaining sugar and leave for another 5 minutes. Serve hot.

Serves 4

Preparation time: 8 mins
Cooking time: 20 mins

Mixed Fruit Charlotte
(Charlotte de Fruits d'Été)

Ingredients
50 g/2 oz/scant ½ cup strawberries
50 g/2 oz/½ cup red and black currants
50 g/2 oz/½ cup raspberries
50 g/2 oz/⅓ cup seedless grapes
100 g/4 oz/½ cup granulated sugar
60 ml/4 tbsp boiling water
7.5 ml/1½ tsp powdered gelatine (gelatin)
100 g/4 oz/2 cups bread, cut in cubes, without crusts
For the sauce:
225 g/8 oz/2 cups raspberries
50 g/2 oz/¼ cup icing (confectioners') sugar
Juice of ½ lemon

Method
1. Clean, wash and drain all the fruits. Place in a large bowl with sugar and hot water. Leave for 1 hour then strain the juice into a saucepan. Bring to the boil and dissolve the gelatine in the liquid. Simmer for 3 minutes. Remove from heat and pour over the fruit. Soak the bread cubes in the fruit mixture without mashing them.

2. Put the mixture in individual moulds. Chill overnight and, when set, turn onto plates.

3. To make the sauce, liquidise the raspberries and icing sugar and strain through a nylon sieve (strainer). Add the juice of half a lemon.

4. Pour a little sauce over and around each pudding on serving.

Serves 4

Preparation time: 10 mins plus chilling
Cooking time: 5 mins

Greengage Pudding
(Clafoutis aux Reine-Claude)

Ingredients
450 g/1 lb greengages
4 large eggs
120 g/4½ oz/good ½ cup caster (superfine) sugar
100 g/4 oz/1 cup flour
5 ml/1 tsp ground cinnamon
300 ml/½ pt/1¼ cups milk
100 g/4 oz/½ cup butter, melted
Icing (confectioners') sugar for dusting

Method
1. Wash, drain and cut the greengages in halves and remove the stones (pits).

2. Whisk the eggs and sugar in a bowl for 3 minutes. Blend in the flour and cinnamon, then gradually stir in the milk and melted butter to obtain a thick batter.

3. Butter individual 150 ml/5 fl oz/⅔ cup ovenproof bowls.

4. Place a layer of greengages in each bowl, cover with batter and dot a few pieces of butter on top.

5. Bake in a hot oven for 20-25 minutes at 200°C/400°F/gas mark 6.

6. Dust with icing sugar and serve with cream.

Serves 4

Preparation time: 10 mins
Cooking time: 25 mins

Sultana Pudding
(Pouding aux Raisins Secs)

Ingredients
60 ml/4 tbsp sultanas (golden raisins)
30 ml/2 tbsp rum
300 ml/½ pt/1¼ cups milk
50 g/2 oz/¼ cup butter
30 ml/2 tbsp white breadcrumbs
2 eggs, beaten
60 ml/4 tbsp granulated sugar
Grated rind and juice of 1 lemon

Method
1. Soak the sultanas in the rum for 10 minutes.

2. Boil the milk and add the breadcrumbs. Stir well. Transfer to a bowl and mix the beaten eggs, sugar, sultanas, lemon rind, lemon juice and butter, reserving 15 g/½ oz/1 tbsp.

3. With the remaining butter grease four pudding basins and fill with the mixture.

4. Place puddings in a shallow dish lined with a double sheet of greaseproof (waxed) paper and half fill with hot water. Bake in moderate oven at 180°C/350°F/gas mark 4 for 30-35 minutes.

5. Unmould and serve with fruit sauce or fresh fruit slices.

Serves 4

Preparation time: 10 mins
Cooking time: 45 mins

Ginger Soufflé
(Soufflé au Gingembre)

Ingredients
50 g/2 oz/¼ cup unsalted butter
60 ml/4 tbsp granulated sugar
(plus little extra for dusting soufflé dishes)
3 egg yolks
30 ml/2 tbsp caster (superfine) sugar
30 ml/2 tbsp plain (all-purpose) flour
5 ml/1 tsp cornflour (cornstarch)
150 ml/¼ pt/⅔ cup milk
30 ml/2 tbsp ginger in syrup, chopped
1 egg, beaten
5 egg whites
60 ml/4 tbsp icing (confectioners') sugar, sifted
4 servings chocolate ice cream

Method
1. Soften the butter and grease the insides of six individual soufflé dishes. Sprinkle granulated sugar inside and turn upside down to remove the surplus. Place on a baking sheet.

2. In a bowl, mix the egg yolks, sugar, flour, cornflour and 3 tbsp of cold milk. Boil the rest of the milk and stir into the egg mixture. Add the chopped ginger. Reboil the mixture for 4 minutes until it bubbles. Remove from the heat, cool slightly and add one raw beaten egg to it.

3. In a clean bowl, beat the egg whites until they thicken but are not too stiff. Blend one third in to the flour mixture then gently fold the rest in with a metal spoon.

4. Fill the moulds to the brim. With a knife make a groove round the top near the edge of each mould. This will help the soufflé mixture to rise evenly without forming a dome.

5. Bake for 13 minutes in a preheated oven at 200°C/400°F/ gas mark 6 on the middle shelf. After 5 minutes check that the soufflés are rising evenly. Otherwise remove and, using a knife, cut the soufflé around the edges. Return to bake until well risen. One minute before removing, dust the top with sifted icing sugar and return to oven for a further minute.

6. Serve immediately with a spoonful of chocolate ice cream.

Serves 6-8

Preparation time: 10 mins
Cooking time: 20 mins

Peaches with Creamed Rice
(Pêche Royal)

Ingredients
30 ml/2 tbsp raspberry jelly crystals
150 ml/5 fl oz/⅔ cup water
100 g/4 oz/1 cup peaches, skinned and sliced or canned
30 ml/2 tbsp pudding rice
300 ml/½ pt/1¼ cups milk, boiled
30 ml/2 tbsp sugar
10 ml/2 tsp powdered gelatine (gelatin)
150 ml/5 fl oz/⅔ cup whipping cream
Apricot jam (conserve)

Method
1. Melt the raspberry jelly crystals in hot water. Pour into four individual ovenproof moulds (molds) (200 ml/7 fl oz capacity) and add a few peach slices to fill the moulds about one-third full. Chill until set.

2. Mix the rice with 60 ml/4 tbsp of water and boil for 6 minutes. Add the boiled milk and simmer for 20-30 minutes or until tender. Add the sugar and gelatine to the hot rice pudding and stir until dissolved. Leave to cool.

3. Whip the cream in a large bowl and fold it into the cold but not set rice. Fill each mould to the brim and chill for 2 hours to set.

4. Dip the mould into hot water and turn out the rice pudding onto a plate to show the jellied peaches.

5. Serve with a little hot apricot jam sauce.

Serves 4

Preparation time: 5 mins plus chilling
Cooking time: 20-30 mins

Zabaglione
(Zabaione)

Ingredients
3 egg yolks plus 1 egg white
100 g/4 oz/½ cup caster (superfine) sugar
120 ml/4 fl oz/½ cup sweet white vermouth
120 ml/4 fl oz/½ cup dry white wine
60 ml/4 tbsp apricot liqueur
Juice and grated rind of 1 lemon
1 sachet powdered gelatine (gelatin)
450 g/1 lb fresh strawberries

Method

1. Whip the egg yolks and sugar together with a balloon whisk until the mixture begins to foam. Add the vermouth, wine and liqueur.

2. Warm the lemon juice and rind and dissolve the gelatine in it. Add to egg mixture.

3. Place the bowl over a saucepan of boiling water and whip for 4 minutes. Remove the saucepan from the heat but keep the bowl on top while whisking for a further 4 minutes until the mixture becomes frothy and sets.

4. Whip away from heat until cold for 4 minutes more.

5. Half fill tall glasses with egg custard. Chill and when set decorate with strawberries.

Serves 6

Preparation time: 10 mins plus chilling
Cooking time: 8 mins

Black Cherry Tart
(Tarte aux Cerises Noires)

Ingredients
225 g/8 oz shortcrust (basic pie crust) pastry
50 g/2 oz/¼ cup soft unsalted butter
1 egg, beaten
50 g/2 oz/¼ cup icing (confectioners') sugar (sifted)
60 ml/4 tbsp ground almonds
30 ml/2 tbsp flour
2 drops almond essence (extract)
60 ml/4 tbsp cold custard
450 g/1 lb black cherries, stoned (pitted)
30 ml/2 tbsp redcurrant jelly (clear conserve)
5 ml/1 tsp cornflour (cornstarch)
60 ml/4 tbsp cold water

Method
1. Brush a 18 cm/7 in round baking tin (pan) with oil.

2. Roll the pastry to a thickness of 5 mm/¼ in, line the tin and prick the bottom. Rest for 30 minutes in a cool place.

3. Cream the butter, add beaten egg and sugar. Blend in the ground almonds and flour. Flavour (flavor) the mixture with the almond essence and blend in the cold custard, making a creamier consistency.

4. Half fill the pastry case with this almond cream. Top up with the cherries and bake in a preheated oven at 220°C/425°F/gas mark 7 for 25-30 minutes.

5. To prepare a redcurrant glaze, boil the jelly with half the water. Blend the cornflour with the remaining water and stir into the boiling jelly to thicken it.

6. Coat the cherry tart all over with the glaze and cool. Serve cold with dairy ice cream.

Serves 8

Preparation time: 10 mins
Cooking time: 30 mins

Plums in Rosé Wine
(Susine al Vino)

Ingredients
900 g/2 lbs firm plums
½ bottle rosé wine
45 ml/3 tbsp honey
1 stick cinnamon

Method
1. Wash the plums and drain. Place in a shallow earthenware dish and cover with wine, honey and cinnamon. Bake in a preheated oven for 20 minutes at 180°C/350°F/gas mark 4. Cool in the wine. Chill and serve when very cold with egg custard or ice cream.

Serves 4

Preparation time: 5 mins plus chilling
Cooking time 20 mins

Peach Sorbet with Brandy (Sorbet aux Pêches au Cognac)

Ingredients
3 egg whites
Juice of ½ lemon
100 g/4 oz/½ cup caster (superfine) sugar
3 large ripe peaches, pulp weight: 175 g/6 oz/¾ cup
150 ml/¼ pt/⅔ cup sweet orange juice
60 ml/4 tbsp brandy
30 ml/2 tbsp sugar
Red food colouring

Method
1. In a clean stainless steel bowl whip 2 egg whites, the juice of ½ lemon and sugar with a whisk for 3 minutes.

2. Place the bowl on top of a saucepan containing boiling water and whisk for a further 3 minutes to poach the meringue. This stabilises the sorbet and prevents ice crystals on freezing. It also sterilises the egg whites.

3. Slit the peach skins and scald them in boiling water. Remove the skin and stones (pits). Add orange juice to the peach pulp and liquidise it to a thin purée. Bring the purée to the boil for 2 minutes.

4. Blend the purée in with the egg whites; beat well to a smooth mixture. Add the brandy.

5. Freeze for 2 hours.

6. Beat the remaining egg white with a fork to make it more liquid. In a bowl, mix together 30 ml/2 tbsp of sugar with 1 drop of red food colouring.

7. Now take four fluted glasses and dip the rim of the glass in the egg white then in the coloured sugar. This will stick to the rim.

8. Allow the sorbet to soften a little outside the freezer for 15 minutes. Beat to a snow and fill the glasses.

9. Pour over a little more brandy or peach liqueur, if liked, on serving.

Serves 4

Preparation time: 10 mins plus freezing
Cooking time: 2 mins

Easter Gâteau
(Gâteau de Pâques aux Poires et Prunes)

Ingredients
450 g/1 lb strong plain (bread) flour
2.5 ml/½ tsp salt
50 g/2 oz/¼ cup vegetable margarine
250 ml/8 fl oz/1 cup milk and water
25 g/1 oz/2 tbsp fresh yeast or 10 g/¼ oz/½ tbsp dry yeast
1 egg, beaten
4 large ripe pears, cored, peeled and sliced
8 large Victoria plums, stoned (pitted)
100 g/4 oz/½ cup caster (superfine) sugar
5 ml/1 tsp cinnamon
30 ml/2 tbsp quince preserve
30 ml/2 tbsp orange marmalade
50 g/2 oz/½ cup pine nuts
Icing (confectioners') sugar for dusting

Method
1. Sift the flour and salt in a large mixing bowl; rub in the margarine until the mixture resembles breadcrumbs.

2. In a small bowl activate the yeast with ½ cup of the milk, at blood temperature, with a pinch of flour. When it begins to froth make a well in the flour and pour in the yeast. Add the beaten egg and the rest of the milk and water, also tepid.

3. Blend well and knead the dough on a floured board for 5 minutes. Cover with a cloth or inverted basin and rest for 30 minutes.

4. Grease a large flan dish, 20 cm/8 in diameter by 4 cm/1½ in deep. Roll out half the dough on a floured board. Line the tin and prick it with a fork.

5. In a bowl blend all the fruits, nuts, sugar and cinammon with the preserve and marmalade; fill the tart.
Wet the edges of pastry (paste) with water.

6. Roll out another round of dough 5 mm/¼ in thick. Cover the tart and brush with beaten egg. Rest for 30 minutes, then bake in a preheated oven at 200°C/400°F/gas mark 6 for 40 minutes.

7. When cooked, dust with icing sugar. Serve hot or cold.

Serves 8

Preparation time: 20 mins
Cooking time: 40 mins

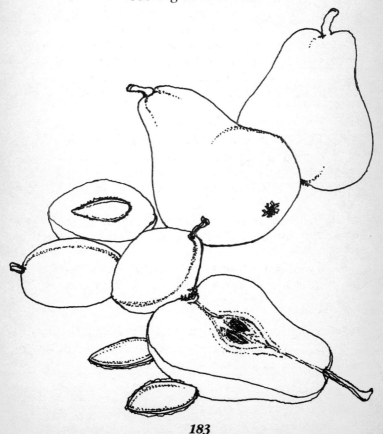

Figs in Maraschino
(Fichi in Spirituo)

Ingredients
8 fresh figs
225 g/8 oz/2 cups fresh raspberries
8 macaroons
250 ml/8 fl oz/1 cup whipped cream
30 ml/2 tbsp maraschino liquor
30 ml/2 tbsp kirsch

Method
1. Cut the figs in halves and place in individual glass bowls.

2. Sieve (strain) the raspberries and collect the juice and purée in a bowl. Crush the macaroons and add to the purée. Stir in the liquor and kirsch.

3. Fold in the whipped cream and spoon over the fresh figs.

4. Chill for 1 hour and serve.

<u>Serves 4</u>

Preparation time: 10 mins plus chilling

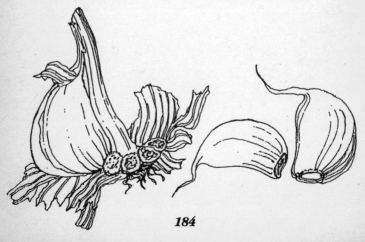

Index